I found Michael Wittmer's book
written, it is easy to understand
laugh out loud. But more importa
oughly biblical, passionate for Christ and the gospel, and outlines
a broad, liberating, and life-affirming perspective that is badly
needed in the world today. Furthermore, it is rooted in sound
scholarship and wide reading. This is popular theology at its
best. I recommend it enthusiastically.

— **Dr. Al Wolters**, Professor Emeritus of Religion and
Theology at Redeemer University College

Michael Wittmer has written a very fine book. In this book,
Mike is practical. In this book, Mike is funny. In this book, Mike
is biblical. In this book, Mike is intelligent. In this book, Mike is
wise. In this book, Mike is down-to-earth (literally). In this book,
Mike is spiritual (literally). In this book, Mike is controversial;
but the so-called "bottom line" is this: In this book Michael is
helpful to the body of Christ. How many stars can I give this
book of Mike's? I will give it five! And that's too low.

— **David Naugle**, Distinguished Professor, Dallas Baptist
University, and author of *Reordered Love, Reordered
Lives: Learning the Deep Meaning of Happiness*

In typical Mike Wittmer style, this book brings clever and read-
able relief to those of us who desire to live a godly life yet detest
the thought of becoming a stodgy, droopy hermit Christian.
With theological precision, Mike takes us on a journey toward a
biblically balanced life. With tons of practical advice, this book
is just what you need to live a vibrant and joyful existence in the
midst of a fallen world. And no one is better to write this than
Mike. I know him personally, and he is the poster child for an
authentic "worldly saint"!

— **Joe Stowell**, President of Cornerstone University

*Becoming Worldly Saints* addresses a topic that is on all of our minds as Christ-followers but we are afraid to talk about. It is an important, though provoking, smart read that is needed in the church today. Chapter 7, "Rightly Dividing the Word," is worth the price of the book alone.

— **Tim Armstrong**, Senior Pastor, The Chapel, Akron, OH

Is it okay for "radical" Christians to play golf while there are unreached people groups? Should Christians ever splurge and go out to eat? Committed Christians struggle with how they should balance Christ's redemptive mandate to go into the entire world and make disciples while still enjoying God-given pleasures of life. In *Becoming Worldly Saints*, Mike Wittmer equips Christians to see life through a crystal-clear worldview in order to be appropriately balanced in their commitments. Wittmer shows in a winsome and engaging style how a proper understanding of biblical theology equips us to wisely make day-to-day decisions: whether considering a call to missions or going to the symphony.

— **Dr. Chris Brauns**, Pastor of the Red Brick Church, Stillman Valley, IL, and author of *Unpacking Forgiveness; When the Word Leads Your Pastoral Search;* and *Bound Together*

This book frees people from viewing this life as though it was the waiting room of heaven. Finally, the church has a book that unlocks the door to understanding how Christians can love life as much as the Author of Life does.

— **Craig R. Jarvis**, Lead Pastor, Medinah Baptist Church, Normal, IL *becoming*

# WORLDLY SAINTS

## Can You Serve Jesus and Still Enjoy Your Life?

# MICHAEL WITTMER

## Foreword by Trevin Wax

**ZONDERVAN®**

ZONDERVAN

*Becoming Worldly Saints*
Copyright © 2015 by Michael E. Wittmer

This title is also available as a Zondervan e-book.
Visit www.zondervan.com.

Requests for information should be addressed to:
Zondervan, 3900 *Sparks Dr SE., Grand Rapids, Michigan 49546*

Library of Congress Cataloging-in-Publication Data

Wittmer, Michael Eugene.
    Becoming worldly saints : can you serve Jesus and still enjoy your life? /
Michael E. Wittmer.
        pages cm
    Includes bibliographical references.
    ISBN 978-0-310-51638-5 (softcover)
    1. Joy—Religious aspects--Christianity. 2. Pleasure--Religious aspects—
Christianity. 3. Christian life. 4. Salvation—Christianity. 5. Salvation—
Biblical teaching. I. Title.
    BV4647.J68W59 2015
    248.4—dc23                                                    2014029375

*Cover design and photography: John Hamilton Design*
*Interior design: Matthew Van Zomeren*

*Printed in the United States of America*

14 15 16 17 18 19 20 / DCI / 20 19 18 17 16 15 14 13 12 11 10 9 8 7 6 5 4 3 2 1

*For James McGoldrick and James Grier,*
*who taught me that redemption is as large as creation.*

# CONTENTS

## PART 3: FALL

## PART 4: REDEMPTION

# FOREWORD

Faithful Christian living involves a paradox: our faith is both world-affirming and world-denying. World-affirming in that we believe the world's structures are fundamentally good, a part of God's good creation now longing to be restored. World-denying in that we believe the world's systems are pervasively evil, firmly opposed to God and His loving rule and awaiting His judgment.

Miss the goodness of the world *structurally*, and you start to think the physical creation is bad, so God must be going to do away with it all in the end. The Christian mission becomes "getting people to heaven," since the world is going to the other place. Miss the badness of the world *systemically*, and you start to think sin is not as serious as we've made it out to be, so tinkering around with things in pursuit of improvement is all that is needed. The Christian mission becomes "make the world a better place."

Careful Christian thinking holds these two truths in paradox, never allowing one truth to drown out the other, never allowing the extreme position of one side to lead us to the other. To miss one side of this paradox or the other is to distort the beauty of Christianity.

The book you are about to read pushes even deeper, reminding us that world-affirming and world-denying Christianity are two sides of the same coin. We won't deny what needs denying unless we affirm what needs affirming, and vice versa. After all, we were made for this world. "We are earthlings, for heaven's sake," as Mike says so memorably. When God created Adam out of the dust of the ground, He put his feet back in the dust and gave Him a garden to cultivate. Humans weren't made for heaven, but for earth. Or more specifically, heaven *on* earth — a world drenched in the presence of the Creator.

Sin, of course, changed everything, so now the world in one sense is structurally a good thing that needs redemption and in another sense is systemically evil and needs to be purged and made right. The truth of the Christian gospel is that through faith in Jesus Christ, we are promised a new heaven and new earth, a place where righteousness dwells, where the new world — both structurally and systemically — is harmonious and purposeful. Those who know and love King Jesus will be with Him forever, not in a disembodied state of shadows, but in flesh-and-blood resurrected and restored bodies.

*Becoming Worldly Saints* conveys truths that are essential for following Christ faithfully. Mike Wittmer doesn't want us to lose sight of the world-affirming aspects of our Christian faith. He doesn't want us to underestimate the power of living an ordinary life of faithful devotion to King Jesus. He doesn't want us to feel false guilt for enjoying the good world God has given us. The truth of eternity doesn't obliterate our earthly experiences; it infuses them with heavenly significance.

Mike is right. It would be a tragedy if we stumble over the extraordinary in the ordinary, the beauty that remains despite the brokenness of this world, and the goodness of cultivating creation in rhythms of work and rest. "This is my Father's world," we sing. "Though the wrong seems oft so strong, God is the ruler yet."

Here is a book that gives testimony to our Maker and the good things He has made. One of the ways we enjoy Him is through *them*. The Father loves to give good gifts to His children, so that our love for His gifts will lead us back to His generous heart.

Mike wants us to be worldly saints. Not flesh-driven or sinful or backslidden, but worldly in the proper sense. Saints who live and move *in this world* — not denying or feeling guilty for our earthly existence, but who see the misdirected idolatry of the fall in this world and who long for redemption in all its glory.

*TREVIN WAX, Managing editor of*
*The Gospel Project, author, and blogger*

# HEAVEN AND EARTH

*Anyone who loves their life will lose it, while anyone who hates their life in this world will keep it for eternal life.*

*Jesus (John 12:25)*

Can you serve Jesus and still enjoy your life?

The spiritual answer is yes, of course. Serving Jesus may be hard, but he offers joy that words cannot express and the world cannot understand. Don't you know that JOY stands for Jesus, Others, and You?

I believe this, though "joy" in other languages doesn't form such a neat acronym — especially in German, in which *Schadenfreude* is not only too long to form an acronym but, even worse, means to take pleasure in another's misery. Leave it to my people, the gruff Germans, to steamroll the joy out of joy.

Still, the short answer is yes. Jesus came so we might "have life, and have it to the full" (John 10:10). Following him is the only way to live. There. Now that we've given the Sunday school answer, the one we know we're supposed to say, can we look at the question again, this time a bit more honestly?

*Can you serve Jesus and still enjoy your life?*

Have you felt the tension between heaven and earth, between what you *should* do because you're a Christian and what you *want* to do because you're human? You would like to lay up treasure in heaven, but you also want to have some fun down here. Have you ever thought you might enjoy life more if you weren't a Christian?

Unless you feel the weight of this question, you'll never understand your nonreligious friends. Most people fear that following Jesus will steal their joy. They are used to living by their own rules, doing what they want when they want, and they're not about to let someone else tell them how to live. Even if he is God.

They'd rather sleep in on Sunday morning, then grab a few friends and head for the beach. Should they pass a church, especially one with stained glass and gussied-up people, they might roll down their windows and blast the defiant anthem of Billy Joel, "I'd rather laugh with the sinners than cry with the saints; the sinners are much more fun. You know that only the good die young. Only the good die young."[1]

***Can you serve Jesus and still enjoy your life?***

Unless you feel the weight of this question, you'll never understand yourself. Why do we often disobey God, doing the opposite of what we know he wants? Isn't it because we're not convinced his way is best, that deep down we suspect life would be better if we did just what we want?

I felt this tug-of-war as a child. I didn't mind going to church on Sunday nights until ABC started a new television series, *The Hardy Boys/Nancy Drew Mysteries*. I read every book in the Hardy Boys series and was enthralled by the trailers of Parker Stevenson and Shaun Cassidy playing the roles of Frank and Joe Hardy. Every Sunday night I went with my family to church, secretly wishing we were heathens so I could stay home and watch Shaun and Parker on my black-and-white TV. The shows must not have been as good as the books, because in three seasons they were canceled.

I did watch *B.J. and the Bear*, another short-lived series about a free-spirited trucker, his chimpanzee, and the beautiful women he rescued each week. Many episodes ended with B.J. rolling down the road, a new fling in his cab, singing along with Billy Joel, "I don't care what you say anymore, this is my life. Go ahead with your own life, leave me alone."[2]

Billy Joel didn't start the fire, but his lyrics stuck in my head and made me wonder if living for Jesus was all it was cracked up to be. Our Baptist heroes were William Carey, Hudson Taylor, and Adoniram Judson, missionaries who had sacrificed everything to bring the gospel to India, China, and Burma. I admired their achievements, but I didn't want to be them. I dreamed of being a tough ladies' man like Thomas Magnum P.I., Ponch and Jon, or Bo and Luke Duke. I knew Jesus wouldn't approve, but part of me pined for the vigilante justice that Kenny Rogers sang about in "Coward of the County." How great would it be, just one time, to take matters into my own hands and punch the thugs out? As Kenny explained, it can be weak to turn the other cheek, for "Sometimes you gotta fight when you're a man."

Could I serve Jesus and still enjoy my life? I wasn't sure. Sometimes I still wonder. Jesus left us with a mission, to "go and make disciples of all nations" (Matt. 28:19). He demands that we go all in, making any and every sacrifice to follow him. He said, "Whoever wants to be my disciple must deny themselves and take up their cross and follow me" (Matt. 16:24). Again, "If anyone comes to me and does not hate father and mother, wife and children, brothers and sisters — yes, even their own life — such a person cannot be my disciple" (Luke 14:26). These are hard sayings, and Jesus encourages us to count the cost before we commit. He may give us time, but he'll give no concession. Jesus doesn't ask for much. He asks for everything (Luke 14:33).

## PLEASURE AND PURPOSE

Recent bestsellers, such as David Platt's *Radical*, Francis Chan's *Crazy Love*, and John Piper's *Don't Waste Your Life*, rightly challenge us to devote our time and treasure to finish this mission of God. What could be more thrilling than standing before the throne of God, surrounded by "a great multitude that no one could count, from every nation, tribe, people and language" (Rev. 7:9), and knowing that some are there because they heard the gospel from you?

I need their reminder that I will someday stand before the judgment seat of Christ (2 Cor. 5:10), and that to whom much is given, much is required (Luke 12:48). This is particularly troubling for me because I don't live in the most target-rich environment for unreached people. I live in America, not overseas; in the suburbs, not the inner city; and just outside Grand Rapids, a city with so many churches that we think we're witnessing when we speak to a Lutheran.

I own a four-bedroom house on a one-acre lot that requires constant upkeep. This week I spent $100 on crabgrass preventer and another $200 for a new heat pump in my basement. I would like to finish my patio deck and build a garden shed, but I'm currently saving for a car. The ratty Civic I'm driving is twenty-three years old — so I'm not exactly a profligate spender — but reading these books makes me wonder if I should duct tape it together awhile longer.

And that's a problem. This excellent emphasis on the higher *purpose of heaven* often stifles the simple *pleasures of earth*. David Platt was convicted that his megachurch needed to slash its budget to free up as much money as possible to help the poor in their city and northern India. They found $2 million, a few hundred of which came from cutting out Goldfish crackers from their preschool ministry.[3]

I applaud Platt and his church for their radical commitment to Christ, but I wonder how they can pull this off without falling into a new form of legalism.[4] I would struggle to justify any purchase — did I really need that coffee, this book, or a new smartphone? — when someone else desperately needs the money. One author confessed that he felt guilty for spending $50 on a discounted suit because the money could have fed a child in India for a year.[5] Something seems amiss when we can't enjoy a cheap suit, not because it's cheap but because we fear we overpaid.

Our lives will shrivel if we allow our passion for redemption to smother the pleasures of creation. Being a Christian must not become an obstacle to being human. But the problem is even worse in reverse: When we eliminate our earthly pleasures, we inevitably limit the reach of our heavenly purpose. If we want to attract people to Jesus, our lives must be attractive. As Howard Hendricks told my seminary class, "If the gospel isn't working for you, by all means, don't export it!"

> OUR LIVES WILL SHRIVEL IF WE ALLOW OUR PASSION FOR REDEMPTION TO SMOTHER THE PLEASURES OF CREATION.

When I was in college, I sometimes had the privilege of driving our chapel speakers to the airport. I was particularly excited to take the evangelist who had inspired us with story after story of leading people to Christ — his waiter, a shoe salesman, even a guy fixing his car by the side of the road. This fellow had "it," and I couldn't wait to get him alone and find out what made him tick. I started our forty-five-minute drive with a soft toss: "How do you find the courage to approach strangers and talk about Jesus?"

The man told a story about leading a man to Christ. Then he told another. And another. And another. Twenty minutes in I realized he wasn't going to breathe. He told the same stories with the same tone he had used in chapel, as if he was preaching on autopilot to an audience of one. I felt guilty that he was exerting so much energy just for me. I felt even worse when I realized I didn't matter. He didn't see me or even care I was there; he was just repeating the same tired lines he had said many times before.

This evangelistic Christian had forgotten how to be human. He was passionate about the high purpose of redemption but seemed clueless about the simple pleasures of creation. He showed no interest in me. He didn't ask any questions about my life, and he didn't tell me anything about himself. I couldn't wait to get him out of my car, which made me wonder about his spectacular conversion stories. How many people prayed the sinner's prayer just to get him to leave?

God calls us to both heavenly purpose and earthly pleasure. These aims often compete. The afternoon I spent spreading mulch around my house was money and time I didn't give to missions. Conversely, the week I spent teaching pastors in Liberia was a week I wasn't home with my family. Heaven and earth may seem to compete, but when we look deeper we find they are actually complementary. A flourishing human life is the best advertisement for the gospel, and the gospel in turn empowers us to become better people.

Can you serve Jesus and still enjoy your life? Let me tell you a story.

# CHAPTER 2

# FABLES

We live in a world where bad stories are told, stories that teach us life doesn't mean anything and that humanity has no great purpose.

*Donald Miller*

**W**hat's your story?

I'm not asking for your backstory: where you grew up, who you married, or what you do for a living. That would be interesting, and if I met you I'd want to hear all of it.

I'm asking about your *big* story, the grand narrative that describes the world and your place in it. This is the story you tell yourself, sometimes subconsciously, whenever you contemplate the meaning of life. Your story has a beginning — where you think you came from; and an end — where you believe you're going. And since it describes both your origin and destiny, your story gives you a pretty good idea about who you are and why you're here.

You may be confused about your big story, especially if you're a Christian living in the West. Spend time online, in school, or at the movies, and you're bound to absorb the modern story of naturalism. This pervasive story says you might as well live for earthly pleasure, for this life is all there is and you only go around once. But then you go to church, where you hear that you were made for something more. This earth is merely a dress rehearsal for your real life, which begins in heaven the moment you die. So downsize and simplify: waste less time on earthly things so you have more energy to lay up treasure in heaven.

**NATURALISM AND SPIRITUALISM ARE TWO EXTREMES THAT DESERVE EACH OTHER. WE MUST REJECT BOTH.**

What's a Christian to do? The rest of this book will explain a better story that embraces both the high purpose of heaven and the normal pleasures of earth. And you'll appreciate this story more if you first understand why we often drive into the ditch on one side or the other. Naturalism and spiritualism are two extremes that deserve each other. We must reject both.

## NATURALISM

C. S. Lewis describes the story of naturalism in his essay "The Funeral of a Great Myth."[1] He says this modern myth, popularized by Charles Darwin, is the story of surprising and spectacular progress. Somehow, "by some millionth, millionth chance," matter and then life emerged from an infinite void of nothingness. Where did this one-celled amoeba come from, and how did it get here? No one knows, but amazingly it managed to replicate itself. Over many millennia and through many fits and starts, it slowly evolved "up to the reptile, up to the mammal." After billions of years and "another millionth, millionth chance," the mammals slowly but surely evolved into humans.

These humans then set about to "master Nature" from which they sprang. They developed culture, inventing "art, pottery, language, weapons, cookery and nearly everything else." They produced airplanes, computers, and Justin Bieber. Who could have guessed all this could rise from that amoebic fleck?

Lewis says this unparalleled story of progress is actually a tragedy, for eventually "the sun will cool — all suns will cool — the whole universe will run down. Life (every form of life) will be banished without hope of return from every cubic inch of infinite space. All ends in nothingness." The universe will fade to black as everything we enjoy — strawberries, chocolate, and strawberries dipped in chocolate — disappears back into the void. The writer in Lewis argues that this tragedy makes a compelling story, but most people think it's depressing. If life ends in death, not just for me but also for the whole universe, then what is the point? I might as well stay in bed and watch reruns of *The Price Is Right.*

Not only does the story of naturalism end in despair, but it also robs life of any higher meaning now. Naturalism declares that physical things are the only things that exist. There is no God, no soul, nothing that is not material. You may feel that you have met your soul mate, but your yearning is merely caused by a rush of hormones or chemical reactions in your brain. You may think you are connecting with God, but that just means the neurons are firing in the part of your brain responsible for feelings of transcendence. You may believe your dog is happy to see you, but really he just wants your food (that one might be true). There are physical explanations for everything. *Matter is all that matters.*[2]

> NOT ONLY DOES THE STORY OF NATURALISM END IN DESPAIR, BUT IT ALSO ROBS LIFE OF ANY HIGHER MEANING NOW.

If naturalism had a theme song, it would be the plaintive cry from the band Kansas, "All we are is dust in the wind.... Everything is dust in the wind." We are nothing but specks of matter blown around by forces beyond our control. All we can do is swallow hard and resign ourselves to whatever fate sends our way. Ultimately it won't make any difference, for if matter is all that matters, then nothing really does.

## SPIRITUALISM

Christians know that naturalism is wrong, but many run so hard in the other direction that they fall off on the opposite extreme. Naturalism lops off the upper story of life, and these Christians respond by brushing aside its lower, earthy side. Naturalism says matter is all that matters, so these Christians declare that *matter doesn't matter* or, worse, *matter is the matter.* They downplay our physical side, saying our bodies are merely temporary residences for our souls or, worse, cauldrons of lust that tempt our souls into sin. If naturalism sings, "All we are is dust in the wind," these Christians chant, "All we are is wind in the dust." That is, we are essentially spirits (wind) trapped in physical bodies.

Christians may be surprised to learn that spiritualism doesn't come from Scripture but from the fertile imagination of Plato, who lived in the fourth century BC. Plato was the student of Socrates and teacher of Aristotle, and like all great philosophers, he tried to figure out the meaning of life. The Greeks before Plato had told various religious myths to explain the origin of the world and how it works. You may remember their stories from junior high: tales of larger-than-life gods, such as Zeus, Apollos, and Aphrodite, who often got drunk, got naked, and tried to kill each other—like Vegas on a really bad weekend. Plato realized that no one believed these religious superstitions anymore, and he set out to explain the world by reason alone.

Plato looked around and concluded that this material world couldn't be ultimate reality because everything here broke down and wore out over time. Especially Fords. Plato posited a higher, invisible world, of which our physical world is just a copy. The higher world, which he called the Forms, consists of eternal, unchanging ideals. Our lower world, which he called Matter, consists of temporary, imperfect copies of those Forms.

Down here we have Fords. Up there is the fixed essence of "car-ness."

Down here we experience kind acts. Up there is the pure form of "kindness."

Down here we have Cleveland sports teams. Up there is "mediocrity."

Plato said that in a previous life our souls lived among the Forms, which is how we are able to recognize cars, kindness, and futility when we see them. The point of life, according to Plato, is to remember that heaven is our true home and not become too attached to this lower, physical world during our brief stay on earth. We should meditate on the higher forms until we die, when our souls will shed our deteriorating bodies and fly back to heaven, where they will twinkle and shine forever.

Here's what you need to know about Plato: he divided the world into two parts and called the upper story good and the lower story bad. Heaven is good; earth is bad. Souls are good; bodies are bad. He passed this dualism on to the Neoplatonist philosophers Plotinus, Porphyry, and Ammonius Saccas (which is also the name of my fantasy football team). Their philosophy in turn influenced Augustine, who is the most important of all the church fathers.

Augustine was a Neoplatonist before he converted to Christianity. Though he checked its most extreme elements at the door, some of its tendencies slipped through. For example, Augustine corrected the Neoplatonist belief that matter was evil, but he still assumed the body was inferior to the higher life of the soul. Since Augustine is the most important theologian in church history, his soft dualism shows up in many theologians who should know better. Consider John Calvin, who often wrote that our bodies are "prison houses" for our souls.[3] Or the distinguished scholar who closed his stirring speech on Christian education with the dispiriting reminder that our educational challenges don't matter anyway because, as an old hymn says, "This world is not my home; I'm just a-passin' through."

Both naturalism and spiritualism are pagan ideas. Neither Darwin nor Plato were Christians, and their big stories miss the meaning of life in extreme and opposite ways. Naturalism affirms our present existence but robs it of any ultimate meaning.

Spiritualism leaves room for the existence of God and a heavenly purpose, but it shortchanges who we are and why we're here.

We are not merely dust in the wind, but neither are we some noble wind trapped in the dust. We are dust, it is true, but we are God's dust. We are the dust of glory. What does this mean, and what difference does it make in your life? Have I got a story to tell you!

# CHAPTER 3

# ONE STORY

The whole gospel for the whole person for the whole world.

*David Naugle*

We often read the Bible as if it were an encyclopedia, looking up passages on parenting, patience, or whatever we're struggling with. As helpful as this can be, a selective reading of Scripture can lead us to easily forget that the Bible, like any other story, has a plot. Its plot supplies the outline for this book and a map for integrating the high purpose of heaven with the normal pleasures of earth.

Scripture's story line is straightforward. Genesis 1 – 2 opens with *creation,* a garden of delight that conveyed but could not contain God's hopes for the world. God created Adam and Eve in his image, empowering them to expand the boundary of Eden until the entire world flourished under their loving care.

THIS, THEN, IS THE STORY OF SCRIPTURE: CREATION, FALL, AND REDEMPTION.

This earthly paradise was shattered by Adam's *fall.* Genesis 3 – 11 describes his rebellion and the curses it unleashed on our broken world. The ground was cursed, Cain was cursed, and finally the whole world was destroyed by a flood. The earth was awash in such violence that God openly wondered if creation had been a good idea (Gen. 3:17; 4:11; 6:5 – 7).

But rather than light a fuse and walk away, washing his hands of our sordid mess, God chose to enter our world and set things right. God initiated his plan of *redemption* in Genesis 12, when he promised Abraham that "all peoples on earth will be blessed through you" (v. 3), and he carried out that promise through the end of Scripture, which closes by imploring Jesus, the divine descendant of Abraham, to return and finish the job.

This, then, is the story of Scripture: creation, fall, and redemption. Some people add *restoration*, but this is redundant, since restoration is already assumed in the act of redemption. Redemption means to buy back, so everything God redeems he also restores. It's better to say that God's story ends in *consummation*, which can be viewed either as the final act of redemption or a discrete step that follows it. The consummation is "redemption plus," meaning that God not only restores his original creation but also lifts it to that higher level it was always intended to reach. I'll say more about the consummation in chapter 21, and much more about creation, fall, and redemption throughout this book. For now I want to highlight how the redemption of creation enables us to integrate the purpose of heaven with the pleasures of earth, or our Christian life with our human life.

### Figure 3.1: The Story of Scripture

| Creation | | Fall | | Redemption |
|---|---|---|---|---|
| *(Genesis 1-2)* | ⇨ | *(Genesis 3-11)* | ⇨ | *(Genesis 12- Revelation 22)* |

## HUMAN FLOURISHING

Most Christians rightly think the "high purpose of heaven" means serving redemption by sharing our faith and making disciples of all nations. We must go above and beyond a routine human existence — work, play, sleep, repeat — for we were made for more than this life. This is true. However, if redemption restores creation, then it's also true that it will not neglect our normal human life. Redemption may do more than restore the pleasures of creation, but it will not do less. And if persistent pleasure comes from finding purpose — note the many aimless retirees who need to be needed — then the heavenly purpose of redemption must also aim to restore the original purpose of creation. The remainder of this book will fill in the details, but here is a broad sketch of how this works.

We learn what it means to be human from Scripture's opening act of creation and what it means to be Christian from its closing act of redemption. If redemption restores creation, then the point of being a Christian is to restore our humanity. All things being equal, no one should flourish like a Christian. We may not drive BMWs or vacation in the Hamptons, but we should thrive in every aspect of our human lives.

Flourishing is a high-minded and hazy term, and since it's a key concept in this book, I must explain what I mean by it. Merriam-Webster defines flourish in two distinct but related ways: (1) to grow luxuriantly, and (2) to achieve success.[1] We flourish in the first sense when we do what is right and in the second when we are rewarded for it. Flourishing in both ways is present when a couple celebrates their golden anniversary surrounded by loving children and grandchildren, when an employee receives a promotion for her diligent work, and when a middle-aged man sheds ten pounds through diet and exercise (he wrote, wistfully).

> A HEART THAT IS LIMBERED UP IN THE DEPTHS CAN EASILY LEAP TO THE HEIGHTS, FINDING DELIGHT IN LIFE'S SIMPLE PLEASURES ... THAT UPTIGHT PEOPLE REGULARLY MISS.

Certainly, doing right is more important than the reward. Proverbs 16:8 says, "Better a little with righteousness than much gain with injustice," and Psalm 37:16 adds, "Better the little that the righteous have than the wealth of many wicked." Doing right is also the only aspect within our control. We can always choose to do what is right, but we can never control the outcome. We may love our family, work hard, and exercise every day, but our much-deserved benefits may be stymied by a rebellious child, vindictive boss, or low metabolism.

Flourishing is a sliding scale. We flourish more or less depending on how well we do and how well we're rewarded. But even when great reward is missing, we may still flourish in the first sense, which has the added benefit of stretching our hearts to more fully appreciate the rewards as they come. I know foster parents who plead with God for an abused child who might soon be returned to her drug-addicted parent. They do not feel like they are flourishing, but I can tell. Their compassion reveals a long-suffering love that can only come from the broken heart of God. I'm jealous, because I know that as God prunes every productive branch so it will bear more fruit, so he uses pain to enlarge our capacity for joy (John 15:2). A heart that is limbered up in the depths can easily leap to the heights, finding delight in life's simple pleasures — the smiling eyes of a child, running barefoot in the park, a tiny hand to hold — that uptight people regularly miss.

## ONE STORY, ONE LIFE

The redemption of creation means that we can't neatly divide our lives into human and Christian categories, here acting in our human capacity and there acting as a Christian. If Christianity restores our humanity, then our human life and our Christian life are the same life. Good Christians make good humans, who then rise to become leaders in the church. Paul told Timothy to find elders who were wholesome, salt of the earth people. Read his checklist and notice how few of these qualities belong to an exclusively Christian category.

> Now the overseer is to be above reproach, faithful to his wife, temperate, self-controlled, respectable, hospitable, able to teach, not given to drunkenness, not violent but gentle, not quarrelsome, not a lover of money. He must manage his own family well and see that his children obey him, and he must do so in a manner worthy of full respect. (If anyone does not know how to manage his own family, how can he take care of God's church?) He must not be a recent convert, or he may become conceited and fall under the same judgment as the devil. He must also have a good reputation with outsiders, so that he will not fall into disgrace and into the devil's trap. (1 Tim. 3:2 – 7)

The only distinctively Christian item Paul mentions is that the man must not be a recent convert, because then he might not be humble, which itself is a generally available human virtue. Everything else in this list — above reproach, faithful, self-controlled, respectable, hospitable, not given to drunkenness, not violent, not quarrelsome, and not a lover of money — are the same qualities we look for in our teachers, presidents, and friends. These virtues are admirable but they're not heroic, which is why it's a scandal when they're missing among Christians.

What should we make of Christians who text while they drive? Who walk about with a perpetual scowl, put down their spouse in public, or scream at their child? Who allow their retriever to rush the neighbors and poop in their yard, put their Disney vacation on a credit card (and then make only minimum payments), cheat on their taxes, waste whole days playing video games or surfing the web, refuse to pay their condominium dues, or waddle back to their seat with their sixth plate from the Chinese buffet?

**IF EVERLASTING LIFE BEGINS NOW, IT SHOULD LOOK LIKE IT.**

None of these are distinctly Christian problems, though Scripture contains principles that speak to all of them. Some of these are worse than others, yet they all reveal at the very least a significant hole in the person's character. Christians who do these things not only throw away their witness — would you want to hear about Jesus from anyone in this list? — but they also miss the point of being a Christian. If everlasting life begins now, it should look like it.

## LIBERATION AND LORDSHIP

How can you tell whether you are integrating redemption and creation, your Christian life with your human life? When you realize that you have more freedom, and more responsibility, than you previously thought.

If the Christian life and the human life are the same flourishing life, then just as Paul searched for wholesome humans to lead the church, so Christians are free to serve God in any wholesome human role. God needs pastors and missionaries. He also needs bankers, dishwashers, and engineers. If God has called you to preach, go to seminary and become the best preacher you can be. If God has called you to be a plumber, start as an apprentice and run all your pipes downhill. Unless it's an emergency, don't try to preach if God has only gifted you to be a plumber. And don't try plumbing if God has only gifted you to preach, because that may create an emergency!

God wants you to enjoy life. He doesn't operate a caste system, so you're not a second- or third-class Christian if you seldom appear onstage in your church. Do what you enjoy doing, do what you're good at doing, and do what the world needs doing. Do it with all your might, following Paul's instruction that "whatever you do, whether in word or deed, do it all in the name of the Lord Jesus, giving thanks to God the Father through him" (Col. 3:17).

It all counts now. This is liberating, because you are free to be yourself. But it also raises the bar, for you must be your best version of yourself. If everything counts, then there are no time-outs in the Christian life. We cannot divide our time or our money: Sunday is for God; Monday through Saturday are for me. This offering is for God; the rest of my money is for me. That's not how it works. God cares how we use our Sabbaths and how we give to his church, but he also watches how we spend the rest of our week and the rest of our money. God yearns for us to read the Bible and pray, but he is also deeply invested in how we talk to our family and friends, do our jobs, and surf the web.

Our Christian and human lives are united because redemption restores creation. Our lives are united in Jesus, who as the Creator of all and the Redeemer of all is also the Lord of all (Col. 1:15 – 20). As Abraham Kuyper put it, "There is not a square inch in the whole domain of our human existence over which Christ, who is Sovereign over all, does not cry: Mine!"[2]

DON'T DIVIDE YOUR LIFE INTO SACRED AND SECULAR, HEAVENLY AND EARTHLY, CHRISTIAN AND HUMAN REALMS. DEVOTE THEM ALL TO CHRIST.

Don't divide your life into sacred and secular, heavenly and earthly, Christian and human realms. Devote them all to Christ, and you will flourish beneath his liberating lordship in every aspect of your Christian and human life. It's the same life, and the only one you have. But it doesn't belong to you. Find your place in God's story. The rest of this book will show you how.

CHAPTER 4

# TWO
# DISTINCTIONS

We Christians care about all human suffering, especially
eternal suffering.

*John Piper*

D id you hear the one about the panda who walked into a
café? He ordered a sandwich, ate it, then pulled out a gun
and shot the waiter. When the injured man asked why, the panda
shrugged and plunked a poorly punctuated wildlife manual onto
the table. "Look me up," he growled as he walked out the door.
The waiter stumbled to his feet and opened the book to the entry
for panda. It read, "Panda: Large black and white bear-like mammal native to China. Eats, shoots and leaves."

This punch line became the title of a bestselling book on
punctuation — yes, you read that right — because it illustrates
the unfortunate consequences of a misplaced comma (the entry
should have read, "Eats shoots and leaves"). A comma is a subtle
distinction, but in this case, it turned a typically docile animal
into an irate, and apparently literate, panda.

Theologians tell a similar, though less humorous story. (You
know you're in trouble when grammarians tell better jokes than

you!) As legend has it, a theologically liberal professor was making the point that God was nothing more than a larger version of us, so he wrote on the chalkboard, "God is other people." This statement bothered a conservative student, and after class he surreptitiously walked to the board and inserted a comma between "other" and "people." Now the sentence read, "God is other, people." Theologians call the student's insertion the "transcendence comma" because it emphasizes the infinite chasm between God and us.

Both of these stories — one funny and the other told by theologians — illustrate how crucial it is to make necessary distinctions. An experienced ear can distinguish the whine of an alternator from the hum of the tension belt pulley, a trained eye knows how to locate the hot from the common wire, and skilled hands can feel the difference between a benign and a cancerous mole. You may not be able to tell the difference between any of these, but aren't you thankful to live in a world with mechanics, electricians, and dermatologists who can?

In chapter 3, I argued that the unity of God's story means we can't separate redemption from creation, the purpose of heaven from the pleasures of earth, or the Christian life from our human life. That's all true, but it's only half the story. We can't separate these things, but we must *distinguish* them. The one story of Scripture means everything matters, but two distinctions within that story show that some things matter more than others.

## NATURAL AND THE SUPERNATURAL

The first and most foundational distinction is what I just mentioned: an infinite chasm exists between the Author of the story and everything that occurs within the story. There is an unbridgeable gulf, at least from our side, between the Creator and his creation.

Take out a sheet of paper, write the word *God*, and draw a line under it. Then put everything you can think of below that line.

*Everything.* Include plants, rocks, dolphins, and people, for we all are creatures who exist below the line. What about souls? They also were created by God, so put them below the line. Angels? Them too. What about heaven? It also goes below the line. Heaven is not a part of God but is the place within creation where God most directly reveals his glory. Even in heaven an immeasurable gap exists between finite angels and their infinite God.

**Figure 4.1: The Chasm between the Creator and His Creation**

| God |
|:---:|
| *infinite, eternal, immutable* |
| |
| Everything Else |
| *finite, temporal, changeable* |

This ontological chasm between God and us has many implications, but I'll focus on just one. If God is alone in his glory above the line, then God is the only being with intrinsic value. Our immutable Creator existed eternally before there was anything else, and he alone assigns value to whatever he brings into existence. What is the meaning of an angel, a human, and a tiger swallowtail butterfly? Whatever God says.

YOU AND I CAN'T CREATE OUR OWN VALUE, BECAUSE WE ARE GOING TO DIE.

You and I can't create our own value, because we are going to die. Solomon wrestled with this depressing truth throughout the book of Ecclesiastes. Every endeavor is meaningless because of death, for "I must leave them to the one who comes after me. And who knows whether that person will be wise or foolish? Yet they will have control over all the fruit of my toil into which I have poured my effort and skill under the sun. This too is meaningless" (Eccl. 2:18 – 19).

Solomon pulled out of his funk when he realized the meaning of life can be found only in the judgment of God. He closed his book by declaring:

> Now all has been heard;
>     here is the conclusion of the matter:
> Fear God and keep his commandments,
>     for this is the duty of all mankind.
> For God will bring every deed into judgment,
>     including every hidden thing,
>         whether it is good or evil. (12:13 – 14)

Your life ultimately matters only because God says it does. Who cares whether you vacuumed under the rug, started your term paper on time, or treated the handicapped child with respect? God does, and he will judge you for everything you ever did. This is terrifying for those who have not wrapped their lives in Christ, but it also assures them that they count. You and your works will live forever, not because you or they are inherently indestructible but only because God will raise you from the dead and reward or condemn everything you've done.

**YOUR LIFE ULTIMATELY MATTERS ONLY BECAUSE GOD SAYS IT DOES.**

The sweeping arm of God's judgment means that everything matters. This leads Paul to encourage, "Whatever you do, work at it with all your heart, as working for the Lord, not for human masters, since you know that you will receive an inheritance from the Lord as a reward" (Col. 3:23 – 24). Nothing is too small to receive God's reward if you dedicate it to him. Nineteenth-century poet Gerard Manley Hopkins explained, "To lift up the hands in prayer gives God glory, but a man with a dungfork in his hand, a woman with a slop-pail, give him glory too. He is so great that all things give him glory if you mean they should."[1]

God's greatness levels the playing field for our works, but it also gives special honor to those activities that focus directly on him. If God is the source of all value, then it is a high privilege to study his Word, speak to him in prayer, and tell others about him. God cares that we flourish in our human lives, but — and these are not mutually exclusive — he cares even more that we know and love him. Jesus said, "What good will it be for someone to gain the whole world, yet forfeit their soul? Or what can anyone give in exchange for their soul?" (Matt. 16:26).

**EVERYTHING COUNTS, BUT SOME THINGS COUNT MORE. THEY JUST DO.**

I want my children to flourish in every way. I hope they read broadly, eat well, exercise, and get along with others. But most of all, I pray that they love Jesus. Everything counts, but some things count more. They just do. If God is the source of all value, then everything matters, and those activities that focus most on him matter most of all.

## CREATION AND REDEMPTION

The second distinction that shows that some things matter more is between God's opening act of creation and his closing move of redemption. Redemption restores creation but only because it is distinct from it. Redemption is to our fallen creation as medicine is to a sick patient. On the one hand, the patient is more important than the medicine, because the whole reason the medicine exists is to heal the patient. But in a moment of crisis, if the patient needs the medicine to survive, then the medicine easily becomes the most important thing in his life.

Imagine a doctor who enters a hospital room with the cure for his dying patient. But rather than inject the medicine into the patient's intravenous line, he tucks the vial into his coat pocket and attempts to minister holistically. The doctor asks the man about the stressors that may have contributed to his disease, what his home life is like, how things are going at work, and whether he knows how to love himself. Before long a shaky hand reaches up and clutches the doctor's collar. "Listen, Doc. Save the chitchat for some other time. Did you bring the cure?"

I've noticed recently that Christians are traveling to other cultures to conduct humanitarian missions. They are going to teach school, dig wells, start businesses, offer medical care, and end human trafficking. These are exciting opportunities, and we should do all of them. I not only applaud these efforts but have participated myself, giving two years of my life teaching English to university students in China.

But we must remember two things: their greatest need and our unique ability. These dear people need education, jobs, vaccinations, clean water, and a fresh start, and we honor God when we help provide these for them. But their greatest need is to know and love Jesus. We rejoice when a young girl is rescued from her pimp, but we're not content until she becomes the slave of Christ (1 Cor. 7:22). We are glad to pay for a local well in an African village, but we pray that its villagers will drink the living water that brings everlasting life (John 4:13–14). We are proud when a student masters conversational English, yet we yearn for her "to grasp how wide and long and high and deep is the love of Christ, and to know this love that surpasses knowledge" (Eph. 3:18–19).

Our humanitarian work has much value in its own right; yet even more, we hope that it provides an opportunity to share the gospel, not only because this is the greatest need but also because

> REDEMPTION IS TO OUR FALLEN CREATION AS MEDICINE IS TO A SICK PATIENT.

this is what Christians are uniquely qualified to do. It is the added value that we bring to any humanitarian effort. Anyone can build a wall, dig a well, or parse a verb, but only Christians can tell people how to be rescued from their sin and live forever.

We must not prostitute our humanitarian work, only serving the poor so we can tell them about Jesus, yet we must not be satisfied until our friends are rescued from all suffering, especially the eternal kind.[2]

**JESUS IS OUR COMMUNITY'S GREATEST NEED, AND ALSO WHAT ONLY WE CAN DELIVER.**

This priority of redemption over creation also applies locally. Christians serve creation and the common good when they go to work, coach a Little League team, or volunteer at the senior citizens center. But none of these should rival the redemptive value they place on church. This summer my daughter joined a gymnastics team. They have ten meets a year, about a third of which may occur on a Sunday. We told the coach that Alayna will come to every practice and every meet that doesn't interfere with our church's Sunday worship. We want her to enjoy her favorite sport, but we *need* her to know that nothing is more important than the body of Christ.

The priority of redemption also applies to the church itself. I am glad when churches participate in the cultural life of their communities, operating rummage sales and food banks, offering space for graduation ceremonies and voting stations, and adopting highways and planting neighborhood gardens. We can do even more, as long as we remember our central mission is to "make disciples of all nations" (Matt. 28:19). Disciples may serve their community in all these ways, but as disciples *of Christ* we will also endeavor to lead our neighbors to Jesus. He is our community's greatest need, and also what only we can deliver. How will people learn about Jesus if not from Christians?

## TENSION KEEPS YOU BALANCED

Have you felt the tension developing over these last two chapters? The unity of God's story means that everything matters, while two distinctions within that story mean that some things matter more than others. Emphasize the unity of God's story (that redemption serves creation) and you may lose the priority on Jesus and his church. Emphasize the distinction between creation and redemption and between the natural and the supernatural and you may wonder how to justify wasting time on anything less than the very best.

Here are two bits of advice that have helped me. First, it's impossible to do only the most important things. Rank these twelve daily activities in order of importance:

Eating
Reading
Cleaning your house
Checking the news
Brushing your teeth
Sleeping
Shaving
Washing dishes
Replying to email
Showering
Reading Scripture and praying
Speaking to family and friends

I hope you didn't spend too much time on this assignment, because it doesn't matter much how you ranked these activities. If you're a normal and reasonably clean Christian, you're going to do them all anyway. Don't worry that you're wasting energy on less important matters; just do whatever needs to be done.

Second, be encouraged if you feel the tension between the natural and the supernatural, creation and redemption, and your human and Christian life. This may be a productive tension, but it's one every Christian should experience. If you ever stop feeling the tension, it means you've fallen off on one side or the other — you're either so heavenly minded you're of no earthly good or so earthly minded you've lost your heavenly purpose.

These introductory chapters have broadly explained the contours of a flourishing human-Christian life. The story of creation, fall, and redemption indicates that everything matters and some things matter more. What does this mean for our day-to-day lives? Let's walk through the story to find out.

# PART 1

# CREATION

This section (chapters 5 – 8) and the following one, "Meaning of Life" (chapters 9 – 13), examine the pleasure and purpose of creation. Although written from a Christian perspective, the content of these chapters applies equally to everyone. Every person is a member of creation, so whether or not they realize it, these chapters describe who they are and why they are here.

This part of the book may not seem sufficiently Christian to some readers. It examines the universal human condition: what it means to be created in God's image and placed on earth to enjoy and steward this world on his behalf. The category of creation is broad enough to embrace every good endeavor; it's the reason why everything you do matters to God.

True enough, but as you read this section, you may find yourself asking, "Don't some things matter more?" The answer is yes, but that won't become apparent until we come to the final act of redemption. Since redemption restores creation, the more we appreciate creation, the better we'll be able to grasp the payoff of redemption. Stay with me as I lay the foundation of creation, and redemption will be even more exhilarating when we come to it.

# CHAPTER 5

# IT'S ALL GOOD

Creation is older than redemption — it is God's first love.
*Scott Hoezee*

I turned the corner and caught my breath. There, at the end of the hall in Florence's Academy Gallery, gleaming from its pedestal in the skylit rotunda, was Michelangelo's *David*. I hurried toward the magnificent statue, but then I stopped. I realized I was walking past something even more interesting. On either side of the hall stood five of Michelangelo's unfinished statues, and the perforated outlines of their emerging forms offered a glimpse of a genius at work. I felt as though I had stepped into Michelangelo's studio, and that at any moment he might return, pick up his hammer, and continue to chisel free the imprisoned figures from their rectangular blocks of marble.

Michelangelo had started one of the statues, *St. Matthew*, to go with a set of the apostles for the Florentine Duomo, and he had begun the other four, aptly called the *Prisoners*, or *Slaves*, to adorn the tomb of Pope Julius II. This project was never completed, and scholars debate whether Michelangelo simply moved on to other things or left the statues unfinished to make a larger point. Perhaps both. The museum placard in front of the *Prisoners* explains that Michelangelo left them half done to express his belief that just as the prisoners' bodies struggle to emerge from the blocks of marble, so our spirits yearn to escape the confines of our bodies.

**IF OUR BODIES REALLY ARE PRISONS, THEN NO ONE CAN BE SAVED.**

Michelangelo's low view of the body is not surprising, as he was a product of his times, and the Middle Ages were deeply influenced by the dualism of Plato.[1] But it is shocking that history's most acclaimed artist held a theology of the body that could not sustain his art. If Michelangelo really believed the physical world was a prison, why did he waste his life painting and sculpting? Why spend years sculpting material statues to convey the spiritual point that the physical world is evil? Didn't he realize his medium toppled his message?

Michelangelo didn't seem to be aware that his low view of the body undercut his career. Even worse, he didn't recognize that it also destroyed his Christian faith. I'm not saying Michelangelo wasn't a Christian, only that the redemption offered by Christianity relies on the goodness of the human body. Evil bodies would make impossible two cornerstones of the Christian gospel: incarnation and resurrection. If our bodies really are prisons, then no one can be saved. Here's why.

## INCARNATION

Christians believe the divine Son could not save us unless he acquired a full human nature, both body and soul. Gregory of Nazianzus explained, "That which he has not assumed, he has not healed; but that which is united to his Godhead, is also saved. If only half Adam fell, then that which Christ assumes and saves may be half also; but if the whole Adam fell, he must be united to the whole nature of him that was begotten, and so be saved as a whole."[2] If you want Jesus to save your soul, then he must have a human soul. If you want Jesus to save your body, then he must have a human body. If you want Jesus to save all of you, then he must have all of what you have, for "that which he has not assumed, he has not healed."

The early church emphasized this point against the Gnostics, heavenly minded heretics who supposed the divine Son would be too pure to sully himself with lower elements like humanity. Many Gnostics committed the error of Docetism (from the Greek word *dokeô*, which means "to seem or appear"), which taught that Jesus was a divine phantom who only seemed to be human. Others said the divine Spirit of Christ entered the human Jesus after his birth and left him just before his crucifixion. Either way, the Gnostics were sure that Jesus could not be fully divine and fully human.

Gnosticism was the first heresy in the history of the church, and it caught the attention of Irenaeus, the church's first theologian. Irenaeus refuted Gnosticism in his work *Against Heresies*, in which he said that as a young man he had known the elderly Polycarp, who as a young man had known the apostle John, who had told him this story. Once John went with his disciples to a bathhouse in Ephesus, but he rushed out when he spotted the Gnostic teacher Cerinthus. "Let us fly," John exclaimed, "lest even the bathhouse fall down, because Cerinthus, the enemy of the truth, is within."[3] We learn from this story that John didn't mind taking baths in public, just not with heretics. Not a bad rule to follow.

GOD, IN THE PERSON OF HIS SON, NOW HAS A HUMAN BODY THAT IS VERY MUCH LIKE YOURS.

John had the Gnostic heresy in mind when he wrote, "The Word became flesh and made his dwelling among us" (John 1:14). Take that, Cerinthus! Jesus Christ, the Son of God, the one you say is too high to dirty his hands with material things, that Son is now entirely and forever human. God, in the person of his Son, now has a human body that is very much like yours.

If you're reading along in John 1, turn back one page to Luke 24. There the risen Christ appeared to his disciples, but "they were startled and frightened, thinking they saw a ghost" (v. 37). Jesus invited them to touch him and see it actually was him, for "a ghost does not have flesh and bones, as you see I have" (v. 39). The disciples still seemed incredulous, so Jesus became a little desperate. He asked, " 'Do you have anything here to eat?' They gave him a piece of broiled fish, and he took it and ate it in their presence" (vv. 41 – 43).

What a pathetic scene! The risen Christ gloriously appeared to his disciples — "Up from the grave he arose, with a mighty triumph o'er his foes!" — and he was quickly reduced to "Look! I'm chewing! See, I can swallow! Somebody touch me!" This humble picture of our Lord proves there is nothing wrong, or even inferior, about having a human body. Jesus has one, and he is right now standing before the Father with it, holding out his scarred hands to intercede on our behalf (Heb. 2:14 – 18; 4:14 – 16; 7:25).

THE INCARNATION IS AN UNFATHOMABLE ACT OF CONDESCENSION, BUT IT IS ALSO GOD'S ENTHUSIASTIC EMBRACE OF THE MATERIAL WORLD.

Besides John and Cerinthus, Irenaeus also mentioned a dustup between Polycarp and Marcion, the first great heretic of the church. Marcion believed that matter was the cause of all evil. He said that Jesus wasn't physically born but just appeared from nowhere as a teenager, in what seemed to be a human form. Irenaeus said that Marcion met Polycarp and asked, "Do you recognize me?" "I do recognize you," Polycarp replied, "The first-born of Satan."[4]

Here's the point, passed from John to Polycarp to Irenaeus and now to you: matter is not the matter. The incarnation is an unfathomable act of condescension — none of us will ever comprehend how God was able to pull it off — but it is also God's enthusiastic embrace of the material world. Jesus' full human nature means God has said YES! to the whole of his creation. God, in the person of his Son, now possesses a full human nature, both body and soul. If the human body is evil, then Jesus cannot have one, and your body cannot be saved. Neither can the rest of you, because of a second cornerstone of the Christian faith: the resurrection.

## RESURRECTION

The Corinthian church contained the most "spiritual" Christians in the New Testament. Some thought they were more spiritual than Paul, for they often spoke in "the tongues ... of angels" (1 Cor. 13:1; see also 2:1 – 5; 14:37). They also believed they were too spiritual for their bodies. Since their goal was to live like the angels, they said single people should not marry, married people should get divorced, and married people who could not divorce should at least stop sleeping with their spouse. Paul replied that while there are benefits to being single, sex is God's gift and married people should have lots of it (1 Cor. 7; cf. 1 Tim. 4:3 – 4).

Worst of all, these angelic elites were too spiritual to believe in a physical resurrection. Their Greek minds were saturated with the otherworldly philosophy that had begun with Plato, and they thought it would be bad for their bodies to rise again. Death would be a welcome release, for it would shed these shells that had imprisoned their souls. Their spirits would now be free to fly to heaven, where they would twinkle and shine forever. Who would want to be reincarcerated in a resurrection body?

This Corinthian heresy seems to be what many contemporary Christians believe. One mainstream publication says, "Our bodies are just houses for our spirit — the eternal part of us that fits in that other dimension. One day we won't need our physical bodies any longer and we will live forever with God in his fantastic spiritual realm."[5] A few years ago, Scripps Howard and Ohio University asked 1,007 American adults, "Do you believe that, after you die, your physical body will be resurrected someday?" Only 44 percent of Protestants and 59 percent of "born-again" Christians said yes.[6] Half of the people in our churches don't believe their bodies will rise again! Their disbelief utterly destroys the Christian faith, as Paul explained to the Corinthians.

Paul reminded them, "If there is no resurrection of the dead, then not even Christ has been raised. And if Christ has not been raised, our preaching is useless and so is your faith" (1 Cor. 15:13 – 14). Paul was so amped to make this point that he took a breath and made another pass, "For if the dead are not raised, then Christ has not been raised either. And if Christ has not been raised, your faith is futile; you are still in your sins" (vv. 16 – 17).

Why did Paul say the resurrection of Jesus is necessary for the forgiveness of sin? In Romans 4:25 he explained that Jesus "was delivered over to death for our sins and was raised to life for our justification." Jesus bore our guilt when he died on the cross, so if he had remained dead he would have remained guilty, and so would we. But the Father vindicated his Son when he raised him from the dead. The resurrection declares Jesus to be innocent, and he shares that vindication with everyone who puts their faith in him. No resurrection means no vindication, which means no forgiveness of sin.

**HALF OF THE PEOPLE IN OUR CHURCHES DON'T BELIEVE THEIR BODIES WILL RISE AGAIN!**

Are you too spiritual to believe in a physical resurrection? Then you are more spiritual than God, who raised his Son from the dead. You're too spiritual to be saved, because Jesus' resurrection is necessary for your justification. You're so spiritual you're not even Christian.

The Christian faith is earthy, physical, and in the best sense of the word, materialistic. Think about the biblical story. It begins in a sensual garden of delight and then tells how a nation was delivered from physical bondage into a land overflowing with milk and honey. The story turns on an embodied God who physically died and rose again, whose sacrifice is remembered in the physical waters of baptism and the bread and the cup. The story consummates on a new earth where, in the presence of God, we will celebrate the marriage supper of the Lamb, bite into fruit from the Tree of Life, and gulp handfuls from the River of Life. From beginning to end, the material world matters.

**THE CHRISTIAN FAITH IS EARTHY, PHYSICAL, AND IN THE BEST SENSE OF THE WORD, MATERIALISTIC.**

The gospel of redemption may be more than creation, but it is not less. Get creation wrong — suggest that matter is the matter or that there is something wrong with this physical world — and you'll never get the gospel right. Creation is not only good, it's also precisely where you belong. We'll look at that next.

# CHAPTER 6

# YOU ARE ALREADY HOME

We are earthlings, for heaven's sake.

*Mike Wittmer*

Everything God created is good, with the possible exception of cats. This goodness of creation is not only essential for the means of salvation — Jesus' incarnation and resurrection — it is also essential for grasping what salvation means. If we suppose we are good souls trapped in bad bodies, then we'll inevitably think of redemption as evacuation. Salvation will turn into escapism, an opportunity to ditch our physical prisons and rise to our true home in the skies.

We'll also never dig deep enough to root out our sin. Listen to people describe their failures — "I didn't intend to click on the racy picture, eat the whole pint of ice cream, or keep the cashier's mistake, but my flesh is weak" — and you get the idea that their poor souls are swept along by the lust that lurks in their bodies. They mean well; they're just no match for their intense physical desires.

Jesus rejected this low view of the material world when he declared that sin comes from the heart rather than from the outside in. The physical world is not our problem, so it's not what goes into our mouths but what comes out that matters. Jesus said, "The things that come out of a person's mouth come from the heart, and these defile them. For out of the heart come evil thoughts — murder, adultery, sexual immorality, theft, false testimony, slander" (Matt. 15:18 – 19). We are not partially good (soul) and partially bad (body) but wholly fallen, both body and soul, from our wholly good creation.

Paul knew that a right view of creation was necessary for understanding redemption, and he told Timothy to preach that "everything God created is good, and nothing is to be rejected if it is received with thanksgiving" (1 Tim. 4:4). Paul was the most important missionary in the history of the church, and it was precisely his devotion to redemption that led him to emphasize the goodness of creation. Get creation wrong — assume our problem is that we exist (as Buddhists say) or have bodies (as Platonists say) — and we'll never understand salvation.

Everything God created is good. I suppose this must include cats, as lions will exist on God's restored earth, where they "will eat straw like the ox" (Isa. 65:25). Cats will live forever on this earth, and so will we.

## NOT JUST PASSING THROUGH

Scripture repeatedly promises that God will restore his originally good creation. Isaiah, Peter, and John all say that our final destiny is a "new heaven and a new earth" (Isa. 65:17; 2 Peter 3:13; Rev. 21:1).[1] The term "heaven" here simply means the sky, where airplanes fly. "In the beginning God created the heavens and the earth" (Gen. 1:1), and in the end he will create a "new heaven and a new earth." Creation, then new creation. Unfortunately, many Christians never reach the "new earth" end of this phrase. They stop at "new heaven" and, assuming that means the celestial abode of God, mistakenly think their destiny is to fly from this world and live forever above the clouds.

I enjoy the tight harmonies and clap-happy rhythms of a gospel quartet, but most have in their repertoire the old standards, "This world is not my home, I'm just a-passin' through" or, worse, "Some glad morning when this life is o'er, I'll fly away.... Like a bird from prison bars has flown, I'll fly away." God's world is a prison? That idea comes from Plato, not Paul — nor Jesus, who created this world and thought he did a pretty good job (Gen. 1:31; Col. 1:15 – 17).

I grew up singing grand hymns that sadly contained some Platonic verses, such as the following:

- "Sweet Hour of Prayer":

  > May I thy consolation share,
  > till, from Mount Pisgah's lofty height,
  > I view my home and take my flight.
  > This *robe of flesh I'll drop, and rise*
  > to seize the everlasting prize.[2]

  What about the Christian hope for the resurrection?

- "A Child of the King":

  > I once was an outcast stranger on earth,
  > a sinner by choice, an *alien by birth*.[3]

  I am an alien to God's good earth, and just because I was born?

- "When the Roll Is Called Up Yonder":

  > On that bright and cloudless morning
  > when the dead in Christ shall rise,
  > and the *glory of his resurrection share*;
  > When his chosen ones shall gather
  > to *their home beyond the skies*,
  > and the roll is called up yonder,
  > I'll be there.[4]

I will live forever in heaven in my resurrection body?

- "Brethren, We Have Met to Worship":

  Let us love and pray for sinners
  till our God makes all things new.
  Then he'll *call us home to heaven;*
  at his table we'll sit down.[5]

  This verse has it exactly backwards, because it says God will take us home to heaven *after* he makes all things new. But if all things on earth are made new, what would be the point of leaving?

This idea that earth is not our home is so widespread that it often shows up in mainstream songs. Secular radio stations play Carrie Underwood's "Temporary Home," which quotes a dying man:

This is my temporary home, it's not where I belong
Windows and rooms that I'm passing through
This was just a stop on the way to where I'm going
I'm not afraid because I know
This is my temporary home[6]

I like Carrie's songs, but have you noticed they can be a little self-serving? When her car is spinning out of control on an icy road, she cries, *Jesus, Take the Wheel!* But when she suspects her boyfriend is cheating on her, she sings she "took a Louisville slugger to both headlights, slashed a hole in all four tires. Maybe next time he'll think before he cheats." How come it's "Jesus, take the wheel!" but not "Jesus, take the bat?" My boyfriend is cheating on me? No problem, Lord. Let me handle this.

All joking aside, I understand why Christians who sing about going to heaven assume that earth is our temporary home. What we sing is what we tend to believe. The catchy tunes bury the lyrics deep in our heart where they're nearly impossible to root out. Even I catch myself humming "I'll fly away" just because it's fun.

But it's still wrong. Genesis 2:7 says, "Then the LORD God formed a man from the dust of the ground." The Hebrew word for man is *'âdâm*, and the word for ground is *'âdâmâ*. God wanted to emphasize our connection to the earth, so he said our name is dirt. If this is true, then the most biblically accurate, theologically correct name you could ever give your child is "Clay." Or "Dusty." If you have a girl, try "Sandy." God made us from the dust of this world. We are earthlings, for heaven's sake.

> GOD WANTED TO EMPHASIZE OUR CONNECTION TO THE EARTH, SO HE SAID OUR NAME IS DIRT.

Some people wonder whether the fall has altered this fact. Perhaps this world was our home in the beginning, but hasn't the wreckage of sin changed this forever? No. If you return home and find that someone has ransacked your place, you will not say, "That's it! I no longer live here! This is not my home!" Instead, you will feel violated because it is your home, and you will immediately set about to put your belongings back together. This is precisely what God is doing for our world.

## THE KINGDOM COMES

An important Christian distinctive is what Jesus taught us to say in the Lord's Prayer: "Father, hallowed be your name, your kingdom come" (Luke 11:2). Every other religion promises to take its followers someplace else. The good stuff is high up and far away, so the goal is to leave this planet behind and go there. Muslims pray to go to paradise, Hindus and Buddhists yearn for nirvana, and Native Americans dream of that "happy hunting ground in the sky" (or as the buffalo refer to it, "hell").

Christianity is the only religion that says the good stuff comes here. Jesus established the kingdom at his first coming, and he will consummate it when he comes again. At that time, "loud voices in heaven" will shout the "Hallelujah Chorus," announcing, "The kingdom of the world has become the kingdom of our Lord and of his Messiah, and he will reign for ever and ever" (Rev. 11:15). The coming of the kingdom is why Paul closes a letter with "Maranatha," which means "Come, Lord!" (1 Cor. 16:22), and why Scripture ends with the plea, "Come, Lord Jesus" (Rev. 22:20). Christians don't pray for God to take them away but for the Lord to come!

Perceptive readers may wonder about John 14:1 – 3, where Jesus said he is going to heaven to "prepare a place for you" and "will come back and take you to be with me." Doesn't this mean that Jesus will take us to live in heaven forever? In Revelation 21:2 – 3 John finished the thought. There he said that when Jesus returns he will bring with him the place that he is preparing. John explained: "I saw the Holy City, the new Jerusalem, coming down out of heaven from God, prepared as a bride beautifully dressed for her husband. And I heard a loud voice from the throne saying, "Look! God's dwelling place is now among the people, and he will dwell with them. They will be his people, and God himself will be with them and be their God."

Yes, Jesus is preparing a place for us. Even better, he is going to bring it to us! Heaven, the abode of God, will come to earth in the end. God is so committed to this world that he will make it his permanent residence. The whole world will be his temple, with his glory streaming from the New Jerusalem, and "the earth will be filled with the knowledge of the glory of the LORD as the waters cover the sea" (Hab. 2:14; cf. Isa. 11:9).

> JESUS IS PREPARING A PLACE FOR US. EVEN BETTER, HE IS GOING TO BRING IT TO US!

This should not surprise us, because one of God's names is Immanuel, which means "God with us" (Matt. 1:23). For most of my life, I read that name backward, thinking it meant "us with God." A friend told me that when the president of the United

States invited him and other religious leaders to Washington, DC, the White House sent advance letters alerting administrative assistants to expect a phone call. Otherwise they might think the call was a prank. What a privilege to be invited to meet the president in the White House! But wouldn't you feel even more important if the president came to your house, slept in your spare bedroom, ate breakfast with your family, and followed you to work? Sure, it sounds a bit creepy, but wouldn't you know that you mattered? And what does it mean that God doesn't merely call us up to where he lives but stoops to make his home forever with us? If this world is good enough for God, it's plenty good for us.

The coming of the kingdom should change the way we pray. I understand why suffering Christians ask God to let them die. Who can blame them for begging God to take away their pain? But even then, the best prayer isn't "Lord, take me!" but "Lord, you come!" When I visited my friend in hospice, her grieving family was simply praying for her suffering to end. She was ready to go and even dreamed that she was approaching the gates of heaven. Together we thanked God for the promise that she would soon see Jesus, but we asked that she would see Jesus not by dying but by his coming. "Please stop her pain," I prayed, "by returning and restoring her body and all creation. Come quickly, Lord Jesus!"

Jesus didn't come that day, and shortly after, my friend died and went to be with him. We are comforted from knowing that she is with Jesus and that this is merely the first leg of a journey that is round trip. Jesus will return and resurrect her body, and she will live with him forever here, on this restored earth. Maranatha!

# CHAPTER 7

# RIGHTLY DIVIDING THE WORD

You keep using that word. I do not think it means what you think it means.

*Inigo Montoya*

Chapters 5 and 6 presented Scripture's compelling case for the goodness of creation. The Bible says creation is good seven times in its very first chapter, and it never lets up. The story of Scripture centers on the incarnation and resurrection of our Lord — two redemptive events that only work if creation is good (John 1:14; 1 Cor. 15:1 – 20) — and it ends by promising physical pleasures of delight on our new, restored earth (Rev. 21 – 22).

Why then are so many Christians suspicious of their bodies and the material world? Because other passages, such as 2 Corinthians 4:18; Philippians 3:20; Colossians 3:1 – 2; 1 Peter 2:11; and 1 John 2:15, seem to say that Christians should seek to rise above the physical world and fill their days with purely spiritual pursuits. But is that really what these texts mean? Would John and Paul argue for the goodness of creation in one passage and then give it all back in another? Would they adamantly oppose the dualism of Cerinthus and the Corinthians only to agree with them in the end?

This chapter will explain how to read these frequently misunderstood passages, and it may be the most important chapter in the book. If you believe what I say here, then your Bible and your life will make better sense. You'll no longer feel a huge chasm between your earthly and heavenly life, between what you want to do because you're human and what you think you're supposed to do because you're a Christian. You will begin to see how both aspects of your life fit together.

## THING VERSUS ACTION

Have you noticed that some words can describe both a thing and an action? The same word can be a noun or a verb. For example, a rock can be a thing we climb on or it can be an action, as in the pregame psych-out song, "We will, we will, rock you!" A hammer can describe a noun that we use to pound nails, or it can be a verb, as in "Don't use Twitter when you're hammered. Your post won't seem nearly as insightful when you're sober."[1]

### 1 JOHN 2:15

This distinction between things and actions is the key to understanding 1 John 2:15, which commands us to "not love the world or anything in the world. If anyone loves the world, love for the Father is not in them." Have you wondered how this fits with John 3:16, which says, "God so loved the world"? This is the same author, John (and God), who told us that God loves the world and yet warned us not to. Is this a contradiction, or at least unfair?

It is neither, because John was using the term *world* in two different ways. In John 3:16 he used "world" as a noun: God loves you and every*thing* he has made. In 1 John 2:15 he used "world" to describe verbs. The next verse explains: "For everything in the world — the lust of the flesh, the lust of the eyes, and the pride of life — comes not from the Father but from the world." What are lust and pride? They are sins, bad actions that God demands we avoid.[2]

So while we must run from the *sin* of this world, we should not ask God, as one pastor prayed, to "protect us from the *things* of this world." He meant to warn against sin, but isn't this an odd way to say it? Consider a Thanksgiving prayer that asked God to protect us from the succulent delights of the turkey and fixings. "Heavenly Father, we implore you this day to guard our hearts from gluttony. Temptation lurks on every side: piles of mashed and sweet potatoes, green bean casserole, fresh bread, salads — both tossed and cranberry, to say nothing of the meat itself and its dressing, nor the ample portions of pumpkin pie, ice cream, and angel food cake that will entice your servants. Please forgive those of us who eat too much and the hands that prepared our temptation. Amen." Wouldn't such a prayer properly end with the speaker wearing the mashed potatoes?

Any good thing can be abused, and the better the meal, the more likely it is that we will commit the sin of gluttony. But we must — and we do — distinguish the delicious meal from its sinful abuse. We thank God for our food and the hands that prepared it, all the while knowing that overindulgence remains a live option. We must carry this Thanksgiving theology into the rest of life, distinguishing the good things of creation from their gnarled form in the fall and refusing to use their abuse as an excuse to dump them.

As Martin Luther told his congregation, just because some people worship the heavenly lights, we don't "pull the sun and stars from the skies." In the same way, just because some people visit prostitutes, we don't "kill all the women"; and just because some people get drunk, we don't "pour out all the wine." (I am Baptist, and actually we do that one!) We still get Luther's point: our problem is sin, not stuff. Luther noted that if we insist on destroying every created thing that might possibly tempt us to sin, we must ultimately kill ourselves, for how often have our sinful desires been fanned by our own perverse hearts?[3]

## 1 Peter 2:11

The distinction between things and actions is also crucial for understanding 1 Peter 2:11, which says, "Dear friends, I urge you, as foreigners and exiles, to abstain from sinful desires, which wage war against your soul." One popular book interprets this verse to mean that "many Christians have betrayed their King and his kingdom" because "they have foolishly concluded that because they live on earth, it's their home. It's not."[4] This is an exceedingly strong accusation. We are committing an act of treason just for thinking this world is our home? God is the one who put us here, so why shouldn't we think he wants us to settle down and enjoy it?

> GOD IS THE ONE WHO PUT US HERE, SO WHY SHOULDN'T WE THINK HE WANTS US TO SETTLE DOWN AND ENJOY IT?

When I was a child, we sang "The Countdown Song." We crouched and counted backward from ten, like NASA launching a rocket. When we hit zero, we leaped into the air and yelled, "Blast off! Somewhere in outer space God has prepared a place for those who love him and obey." The song was a lot of fun for us kids, but the lyrics now seem a little bizarre. Our true home is in outer space? Really?

I call this Martian theology. We sound like a cult — remember the members of Heaven's Gate, who believed the Hale-Bopp comet would whisk them away from the earth? We sound that strange to our non-Christian neighbors when we insist that we don't belong on this planet. I met a man who passes out a business card with the cartoon character "Marvin the Martian" alongside 1 Peter 2:11 and the phrase, "I'm just an alien waiting to go home." Does this strike anyone else as more than a little weird?

Look again at 1 Peter 2:11. What kind of alien does Peter say we are? We are "foreigners and exiles" to "sinful desires." We are moral aliens, strangers to the sin of this fallen world. We're not alien things, heavenly beings who don't belong on planet Earth.

As humans we should be comfortable with the *things* of this world. God created us to breath oxygen, eat food, and contribute to the overall health of the planet. As Christians we must oppose the *bad actions* of this world. It's the sin of this world — not its stuff — that should drive us nuts.

> **AS HUMANS WE SHOULD BE COMFORTABLE WITH THE *THINGS* OF THIS WORLD.**

## COLOSSIANS 3:1 – 2

The same distinction between things and actions is at play in Colossians 3:1 – 2, which urges, "Since, then, you have been raised with Christ, set your hearts on things above, where Christ is, seated at the right hand of God. Set your minds on things above, not on earthly things." Many Christians think these verses mean they should spend as little time as possible on physical, earthly matters so they have more time for spiritual, heavenly pursuits. It may not be a sin to have a garden, play basketball, or watch a movie, but God is more pleased when they read Scripture, pray, and share their faith.

I agree that we must study Scripture and talk to God in prayer, but I disagree that this is what Paul was saying here. In verse 5 he said to "put to death, therefore, whatever belongs to your earthly nature," and in Greek the phrase "earthly nature" is exactly the same as "earthly things" in verse 2. Then Paul went on to tell us what these earthly things are that we must avoid: "sexual immorality, impurity, lust, evil desires and greed, which is idolatry ... anger, rage, malice, slander, and filthy language.... Do not lie to each other" (vv. 5 – 9). What are these things? They are not things at all, but sins. So when Paul said don't set your heart on earthly things, he simply meant don't set your heart on sin.

Likewise, heavenly things turn out to be a grocery list for acts of righteousness. Paul explained: "Therefore, as God's chosen people, holy and dearly loved, clothe yourselves with compassion, kindness, humility, gentleness and patience. Bear with each other and forgive one another if any of you has a grievance

against someone. Forgive as the Lord forgave you" (vv. 12 – 13).
How do you know that you have set your mind on things above?
When you respond to the slights and selfishness of a fallen world
with kindness, patience, and compassion.

## PHILIPPIANS 3:20

The thing-versus-action distinction is also significant for understanding Philippians 3:20, which says "our citizenship is in
heaven." This does not mean we are supposed to live in heaven,
for the word "citizenship" does not describe our physical location
but our allegiance, which is a moral category. When I lived in
China, I remained a citizen of America. My national loyalty was
to the USA even though I was living someplace else. Likewise,
Paul was writing to Roman citizens living in Philippi, and he
was telling them that just as their primary political allegiance
was to faraway Rome, so their allegiance that trumped all other
loyalties was to heaven, where God's will is unwaveringly followed. It is clear that Paul didn't mean to say heaven is our home,
because he said Jesus is coming "from there" to "transform our
lowly bodies," and resurrection bodies belong on the renovated
earth rather than in an ethereal heaven (3:20 – 21).

Here's the point: whenever you read in Scripture such terms
as *world, foreigner, exile, alien, citizen, things above, things below,*
or *heavenly things* and *earthly things*, stop and ask whether these
words are describing things or actions, nouns or verbs. The context will always tell you.

## CONTEXT

Context is particularly crucial for the most frequently misunderstood passage on this topic. Paul declared in 2 Corinthians 4:18,
"So we fix our eyes not on what is seen, but on what is unseen,
since what is seen is temporary, but what is unseen is eternal." If
you look at this verse by itself, it seems to be a straightforward
statement of Plato's dualism: we should focus on spiritual pur-

suits because they last forever and pay less attention to physical objects because they don't. I once heard this passage used just this way on Easter. On the day when we celebrate the physical resurrection of our Lord, the fact on which our Christian faith depends, the preacher cited this passage to warn us against the frivolity of the physical!

Whenever I hear this verse in sermons, it is usually followed by a variation of the following: "There are only two things that last forever, the Word of God and souls. Everything else is going to burn, so live for what matters most!" One pastor explained, "You will not be in heaven two seconds before you cry out, *Why did I place so much importance on things that were so temporary? What was I thinking? Why did I waste so much time, energy, and concern on what wasn't going to last?*"[5]

I appreciate the sentiment, though I've never heard a balding, middle-aged man lament the many hours he washed his hair as a teenager or a weary mother mourn the fact that her family ate all of her Christmas dinner. "I worked all morning on my ham dinner, and now it's gone! What a waste!" Many things that don't last forever are still worth our time. More important, I'm convinced this is not Paul's point in 2 Corinthians 4:18.

In context, Paul was bemoaning his persecution. He said, "We are hard pressed on every side, but not crushed; perplexed, but not in despair; persecuted, but not abandoned; struck down, but not destroyed. We always carry around in our body the death of Jesus" (2 Cor. 4:8 – 10). But he added, "We do not lose heart. Though outwardly we are wasting away, yet inwardly we are being renewed day by day. For our light and momentary troubles are achieving for us an eternal glory that far outweighs them all" (4:16 – 17).

Where in the biblical story of creation, fall, and redemption would you put Paul's persecution and the deterioration of his body? Wouldn't you say it's a consequence of the fall? And what about his "eternal glory," the flourishing soul that is being renewed because he is responding the right way? Wouldn't you put it in redemption? Now read verse 18, in context: "So we fix our eyes not on what is seen [*the fall*], but on what is unseen [*redemption*], since what is seen [*the fall*] is temporary, but what is unseen [*redemption*] is eternal."

**WE WON'T FIND ONE NEGATIVE WORD ABOUT CREATION ANYWHERE IN SCRIPTURE.**

This verse is speaking entirely about the fall and redemption. There isn't one word here about creation! Yet I have only ever heard this verse used to put down the physical world — if you can see it, touch it, taste it, or kick it, then it isn't worth your time — when actually the topic of creation doesn't even come up! Paul was not channeling Plato's disdain for material things but was simply encouraging us to focus on the payoff of redemption, which will long outlast anything the fall can dish out.

When read correctly, in context and with attention to how words are used, we won't find one negative word about creation anywhere in Scripture. And why would we? Scripture opens with the goodness of this physical world, relies on that goodness to perform the saving acts of the incarnation and resurrection, and culminates with the material pleasures of a redeemed earth. God is pro-creation (it's okay if that sounds like procreation, because sex was his idea too), and he wants us to enjoy it. We'll examine what this means for us next.

# CHAPTER 8

# WHERE DO YOU ENJOY GOD'S WORLD?

Christ plays in ten thousand places.

*Gerard Manley Hopkins*

The payoff to learning that creation is good and the earth is our home is simple: enjoy God's world! You not only have God's permission, but you have his blessing to delight in the nature, culture, and people that envelope your life.

Pause for a moment and listen. What do you hear? Birds singing their morning lines, the low growl of a bus as it lurches from its stop, the whirling white noise of a fan, or children fighting for their turn with a hand-me-down bike? Ponder the wonder of being *here*. You are alive, and you are on earth, an entire planet of intriguing people and places to explore. Honestly, where else would you rather be? Perhaps a spa, especially if you can still hear those kids, yet that also is a place on earth.

What wholesome thing would you like to do today? Go do it, and feel God's pleasure as you take pleasure in this world he prepared for you.

This encouragement is hard for some Christians to accept. One elderly lady approached my colleague after his sermon on the goodness of creation and asked, "So what you're saying is that when I putter around in the garden, God is okay with that?" I groaned when I heard this story. Here is a dear saint who loves Jesus and loves gardening and didn't know how to bring them together. She thought Jesus might grant her a small garden, not too large that it would distract from her heavenly calling, and even then she felt guilty that time spent in her roses and peonies was time away from her Lord.

Why do earnest Christians often feel guilty when they enjoy creation? Some might miss the point of the passages we examined last chapter, while others rightly feel the tension of the two distinctions we explored in chapter 4. How can they justify spending time and money on creation when redemption is in play? Won't concern for the natural world prevent them from valuing the infinitely more important supernatural realm of God?

## THE DANGER OF FRIVOLITY

I once spoke with a friend who thought I might have overplayed the importance of creation. When I asked what he meant, he said, "Take sports as an example. I think Jesus might have played games with the neighborhood kids when he was a child, but once he became a teenager he would have become focused on more important matters." I thought this was an interesting comment coming from my friend, because he both watches and plays a lot of sports. He is also a respected leader in his church, and he was inadvertently admitting he didn't know how to reconcile his love for Jesus with his passion for sports.

It is a tribute to my friend that he raised this issue, for the tension between the common play of creation and the special purpose of redemption only troubles committed Christians. If you have never wondered whether your day bass fishing or visiting the amusement park or bluegrass festival might have been better spent (the answer to that last one is definitely yes), then you may have lost sight of your redemptive mission altogether. I'm proud of my friend for asking the question.

And yet I disagree with his premise that an adult Jesus would have been too spiritually mature to enjoy the normal pleasures of creation. We don't know much about his life before he turned thirty and began his ministry (Luke 3:23), so this is an argument from silence, but it seems that Jesus did not spend his twenties on solely redemptive activities. At least whatever he did then was not considered significant enough to include in any of the four Gospels. Even after Jesus began his ministry, he still made time for long and raucous dinners, so much that he was accused of being "a glutton and a drunkard, a friend of tax collectors and sinners" (Matt. 11:19). It might be hard to imagine a sweaty Jesus kicking a ball to a cutting teammate, but it's even more difficult to picture him enjoying a party with "tax collectors and sinners," which would have included prostitutes, adulterers, and thieves (Matt. 9:11). We know he did the latter, so why not the former?

Jesus' parables also demonstrate a deep engagement with creation. He drew material from his knowledge of farming, fishing, flowers, and fowl, just to name a few (phew!). His stories reveal his experience with baking, traveling, money, management, and workplace politics. Jesus packed a lot of living into thirty-some years, and he used his immersion in the ordinary acts of creation to support his mission of redemption. Jesus continued to practice his creation skills even after his resurrection. When the risen Lord wanted to restore his relationship with Peter, he prepared his friend for their difficult conversation by making breakfast on the beach. Jesus' scarred hands built a fire and baked some bread and fish, which he passed out to his disciples (John 21:9 – 14).

> THE RISEN CHRIST REMAINS FULLY HUMAN, SO I'M ALLOWED TO BE HUMAN TOO.

The risen Christ remains fully human, so I'm allowed to be human too. I don't have to be one of those exhausting people whose spiritual switch is stuck in the On position. I'm thinking of those people who say, "Praise the Lord," just to clear their throats and wedge Jesus into every conversation, even when he doesn't naturally fit. "Yes, I would like a piece of pie, and in return, I would like to offer you peace of mind. Do you know Jesus?" They have stamped their life in Christianese: Every tweet is a Bible verse or inspirational saying that they once decoupaged and hung on their wall; their minivan has a decal of Calvin and Hobbes bowing before the cross and a fish symbol gobbling up other fish with evolved feet; and they're sporting the tattoo "Jesus is my Savior," which, depending on the level of wrinkle and sag, might someday read, "Jesse is my salad."

**A GOOD LIFE IS LIKE GOOD JAZZ: IT HAS RHYTHM.**

These actions aren't wrong, but they're also not necessary. If redemption restores creation, creation has value in its own right. A good life is like good jazz: it has rhythm. The best lives alternate between creation and redemption, family and church, work and play. They integrate these spheres even as they keep them distinct, knowing that if they aren't distinct, there is nothing to integrate. Yes, we must pray for opportunities and always be on the lookout to make disciples for Christ. But we should also feel God's pleasure when we enjoy unnecessary, extravagant moments of worldly pleasure, like breakfast on the beach. Jesus made time for this, right before he returned to heaven.

## THE DANGER OF IDOLATRY

Besides the fear that we might undervalue redemption, some Christians worry that enjoying creation might easily lead to idolatry. The more toys we accumulate, the more our hearts may become bogged down by "the worries of this life, the deceitfulness of wealth and the desires for other things" (Mark 4:19). These Christians are right to be concerned, as God warned Israel that their biggest test would come from success. He cautioned them upon entering the Promised Land:

> Be careful that you do not forget the LORD your God, failing to observe his commands, his laws and his decrees that I am giving you this day. Otherwise, when you eat and are satisfied, when you build fine houses and settle down, and when your herds and flocks grow large and your silver and gold increase and all you have is multiplied, then your heart will become proud and you will forget the LORD your God, who brought you out of Egypt, out of the land of slavery. (Deut. 8:11 – 14)

We sinners too often use God's gifts to lead us away from him. John Calvin observed that we are "a perpetual factory of idols," and we need to be continually reminded that our ultimate satisfaction cannot be found in anything less than God.[1] This is why I benefit from reading Jonathan Edwards, one of America's greatest theologians, who emphasized that "the happiness of the creature consists in rejoicing in God, by which also God is magnified and exalted."[2] God alone must be our ultimate desire and highest joy. We must never allow any good thing to supplant his rightful place in our lives.

However, our struggle to avoid idolatry can easily lead us to fall off the other side and improperly diminish the gifts of God's world. Creation may be relative, but it is real. A ham sandwich does provide a window through which we enjoy God — the ultimate end of all things — but it's also a sandwich that we can enjoy for its own sake. Sometimes a sandwich is (mostly) just a sandwich.

There are two ways to ruin our relationship with the Giver of all things. The first is to ignore him and focus entirely on his gifts. This temptation to idolatry is ever present, and we must remain vigilant against it. The second way is to ignore the gift and focus entirely on the Giver. What would we make of an insufferably pious child who opened every Christmas present only to toss it aside and say, "Thanks, Mom and Dad, but all I really want is you!" Wouldn't the parents throw up their hands and say, "I'm glad you love us best, but you know what, you're impossible to shop for!" If the first temptation ignores the *God who gives*, the second refuses to let him be the God *who gives*.

This latter temptation is a subtler form of idolatry. It's idolatry because we are acting as if we know better than God, who gives us "every good and perfect gift" to enjoy (James 1:17). Theologian Doug Wilson explains, "If I turn every gift that God gives over in my hands suspiciously, looking for the idol trap, then I am not rejoicing before Him the way I ought to be."[3] And it's subtle because it seems exceedingly pious. We assume we must be in pretty good shape if our biggest problem is that our love for God swamps our appreciation for his gifts. Can we really love God too much?

No, but we can piously destroy our ability to love him at all. Every healthy marriage requires a lover and a beloved, two distinct persons who come together as one. While unity is the goal of marriage, husbands and wives quickly discover they cannot achieve oneness without maintaining some personal distinction. When they spend time apart, cultivating their own vocation and interests, they find they have more to love the other person with. As a country song humorously put it, "How can I miss you when you won't go away?"[4] Love may overcome any distance, but it cannot exist without some distance to overcome. You can't love the other if there is no other.

And that's the danger here. If we make too little of creation — if we don't enjoy the world as the world — we may lose our grip on its real yet relative existence. And without a real existence, distinct from yet dependent on God, we will have no place to stand to love God from. We and everything else will be subsumed into him.

Jonathan Edwards himself may have slid down this slippery slope. While he rightly reminded us that our ultimate end is to rejoice in the glory of God, he mistakenly elevated God's glory by diminishing the existence of everything else. Many scholars believe Edwards succumbed to panentheism, the view that the entire world actually exists within God. You and I and peach pie only exist as thoughts in the mind of God. Edwards explained, "God contains, envelops, all other reality … as a consciousness contains that of which it is conscious," so that "the whole is *of* God, and *in* God, and *to* God."[5]

This is dangerously unbiblical. Scripture teaches that creation exists separately yet dependently on God. Adam and Eve were able to love God only because they were distinct from him. They communed with God when he came down to walk with them, but they also spent time apart, naming the animals, gardening, and having sex. Likewise, on the new earth we won't just stand there, staring adoringly at Jesus forever and ever. We will thrill to worship him, but we will also do what normal humans do. According to Isaiah 65:21, on the new earth "they will build houses and dwell in them; they will plant vineyards and eat their [nonalcoholic] fruit" (that's my Baptist version).

We must see God's gifts of creation as windows into his glory and opportunities to praise him. But we must also find pleasure *in them*. We should thank God for our day on the lake, but we don't need to say, "Praise you, Jesus!" with each cast. We must thank God for our daily bread, but it's okay to focus on the flavors of our sandwich while we're eating it. We're even allowed to score a touchdown or hit a home run without pausing to pound our chest and point to heaven.

> WE MUST SEE GOD'S GIFTS OF CREATION AS WINDOWS INTO HIS GLORY AND OPPORTUNITIES TO PRAISE HIM. BUT WE MUST ALSO FIND PLEASURE *IN THEM.*

Our love for Jesus and his world is not a zero sum game. Attention given to creation is not stolen from its Creator. The more we enjoy God's gifts for their own sake, the more we can appreciate him. And thank him for, and love him with. Where will you enjoy God's creation today? Thank God for the privilege of being human and of being here. Then go have some fun.

# PART 2

# THE MEANING OF LIFE

The meaning of life is revealed in Scripture's opening scene of creation. Until now this book has contrasted the high *purpose* of redemption with the normal *pleasures* of creation. While this is a helpful distinction, it disguises the fact that creation has purposes too. And since creation was here first, its goals are more foundational than the goals of redemption. If redemption restores creation, the purpose of redemption must be to restore the purposes of creation.

Many Christians mistakenly try to discover the meaning of life by starting at the end of the biblical story, with redemption. They say, "I'm saved; what is the meaning of my Christian life?" They come up with a narrow set of distinctively Christian goals, concluding that we exist exclusively for worship, ministry, fellowship, evangelism, and discipleship.[1] These are essential activities for every Christian. However, they only cover a sliver of our lives. Most of us can't spend more than 10 percent of our time in church and parachurch activities.

C. S. Lewis observed that coming to Jesus didn't change so much *what* he did but *how* he did them. He wrote, "Before I became a Christian I do not think I fully realised that one's life, after conversion, would inevitably consist in doing most of the same things one had been doing before, one hopes, in a new spirit, but still the same things."[2] Christian or not, you're going to spend most of your life hanging out with family and friends, going to work, cooking dinner and cleaning up, and any number of things you do not because you're Christian but simply because you're human.

How do these activities fit into the meaning of life? To find out, we must start at the beginning of the biblical story, with creation. Rather than ask, "I'm *saved*, what is the meaning of my *Christian* life?" we must ask the broader question, "I'm made in the *image of God*, what is the meaning of my *human* life?" Then we will discover a list of purposes that is as large as life itself. We exist to love God, serve neighbor, responsibly cultivate the earth, and rest every seven days. Every thought you will ever have and every action you will ever do falls into at least one of these categories. The ensuing chapters will examine each one individually, starting with worship, our need to know and love God.

CHAPTER 9

# LOVE GOD

Jesus Christ is the key to the secret of creation.

*Karl Barth*

Every month half a million people Google the question, "What is the meaning of life?" And that's just Michigan fans. The first statement is true, and the second kills in the state of Ohio, where I'm from. Wherever you live, there is a good chance that you or someone you know has wondered what life is all about. And despite what the song says, you don't think it's the hokey-pokey.

If you've spent any time in church, you know that the answer to the meaning of life question is clear: We're here to know and love God. But if you've spent any time in this book — and since you're reading chapter 9, I'm assuming you have — then you already know that the answer may not be so simple. Our love for God contains a fruitful tension. I'll let Jesus explain.

## PEARL

Jesus said the kingdom of God is like treasure hidden in a field or a pearl of great value. When a man discovered the treasure or found the pearl, he quickly sold everything he had to scrape together enough money to buy it (Matt. 13:44 – 46). Nothing in this life is more important than loving God, for "What good will it be for someone to gain the whole world, yet forfeit their soul? Or what can anyone give in exchange for their soul?" (Matt. 16:26).

We need to ponder this question every day, lest we become worldly (in the sinful sense of that word). Our secular culture urges us to find ultimate satisfaction in the things of this world. Its message finds fertile soil in our fallen hearts. From the moment we acquired object permanence, we sought our permanence in objects. At first we cried for a cupcake. If only we could have a second one, we knew we would be happy. Then we yearned for a doll or a bike. Later we thought we'd be satisfied if only we had a car, a date, the right college, and then a spouse. As we matured, we thought it would only take a career, a house, children (what were we thinking?), grandchildren (that's better), then early retirement. One woman told me that with the rise of gourmet bakeries, she has circled all the way back to cupcakes!

> THE THING WE HOPE IS GOING TO MAKE US HAPPY ALWAYS LIES JUST BEYOND OUR GRASP.

Have you noticed a trend? The thing we hope is going to make us happy always lies just beyond our grasp. We are temporarily thrilled when we finally get it, but soon we realize that wasn't it, and we're off in pursuit of the next big thing. When will we learn? If everything until now hasn't delivered the satisfaction it promised, why would we think the next thing will? If, as the advertisement says, a Snickers chocolate bar really satisfies, then why are we so fat?

Don't take my word for it. Listen to the people who have achieved the dream. King Solomon had everything a man could want and a little more. He actually had too much. Can you imagine the drama that came with seven hundred wives and three hundred concubines (1 Kings 11:3)? Solomon sought satisfaction in wine, projects, gardens, music, and excessive wealth. He said, "I became greater by far than anyone in Jerusalem before me.... I denied myself nothing my eyes desired; I refused my heart no pleasure." And yet he concluded, "Meaningless! Meaningless!... Utterly meaningless! Everything is meaningless" (Eccl. 2:9 – 10; 1:2).

Listen to Tom Brady. This American hero has cover-boy good looks, is married to super-model Gisele Bündchen, and has led the New England Patriots to three NFL championships. His new $20 million California house is surrounded by a moat! But it's still not enough. Brady confessed during an interview, "Why do I have three Super Bowl rings and still think there's something greater out there for me? I mean, maybe a lot of people would say, 'Hey man, this is what is.' I reached my goal, my dream, my life. Me, I think, 'God, it's got to be more than this.' I mean this isn't, this can't be what it's all cracked up to be."

> AUGUSTINE LEARNED THAT THE MORE HE SCRATCHED HIS DESIRES, THE MORE HE ITCHED.

The interviewer asked, "What's the answer?" Brady responded, "I wish I knew. I wish I knew."[1]

Brady and Solomon both discovered that nothing in this life ultimately satisfies. It's not supposed to. Augustine famously opened his *Confessions* by telling the Lord, "You have made us for yourself, and our heart is restless until it rests in you."[2] As a sexually promiscuous speechwriter for the emperor, Augustine enjoyed all the pleasures and success a man could want. Yet he learned that the more he scratched his desires, the more he itched.

> THE ONLY THING THAT WAS EVER MEANT TO SATISFY YOU IS GOD.

You and I may never win a lifetime achievement award, enter a Hall of Fame, or see our name in lights. So it's good to hear from those at the top that celebrity, money, or anything else is absolutely not worth the climb. As you grasp for the next rung, remember that ultimately it doesn't matter if you rise or fall. The only thing that was ever meant to satisfy you is God.

## YEAST

But loving God alone is not enough either. Jesus told another parable: "The kingdom of heaven is like yeast that a woman took and mixed into about sixty pounds of flour until it worked all through the dough" (Matt. 13:33). Do you hear the tension between these dueling parables? God and his kingdom are the pearl that is worth more than the world. But the kingdom is also yeast that permeates the world and causes it to rise.

When you love someone, you tend to take an interest in what they love. Because I love my children, I know more Pop-Tart flavors and Taylor Swift songs than a grown man should. And because I love God, I must also love what he loves. What does God love? The world (John 3:16). There's the rub. We must love God more than the world, yet if we truly love God, we will also love the world, on his behalf. God matters more than the world, but because he loves it, the world now matters.

I sing the hymn, "Turn your eyes upon Jesus; look full in His wonderful face, and *the things of earth will grow strangely dim*, in the light of His glory and grace."[3] This is a wonderful statement of the kingdom as pearl, but we need to add a second version of the chorus that emphasizes that the kingdom is also yeast: "Turn your eyes upon Jesus; look full in His wonderful face, and the things of earth will grow strangely *significant*!"

Here's the point: God must be number one in our lives, but he must also be more than that. If God is merely number one, then we can check him off. We awake and have our devotions first thing. Check! The rest of the day is for us. We give God an offering right off the top. Check! The rest of the money is for us. We set aside the first day of the week for worship. Check! The rest of the week is for us.

God must be more than merely our top priority; he must also permeate our lives. God and his kingdom are like the hub of a wheel, and the spokes that penetrate outward must transform every aspect of our lives. God cares deeply that we read our Bible, pray, worship, and support our local church. He also cares how we talk to our family, what we do for fun, and how we perform our jobs. We must remember this daily lest we become worldly from the other side.

> GOD MUST BE MORE THAN MERELY OUR TOP PRIORITY; HE MUST ALSO PERMEATE OUR LIVES.

We become worldly when we fail to love God more than the world (pearl), and we become worldly when we fail to serve the world on God's behalf and live as those who don't know God (leaven). The latter happens when Christians compartmentalize their lives. They know God cares about the eternal, spiritual stuff, but they don't think he cares so much about temporal, physical matters. They're careful to store up treasures in heaven even as they blow through their responsibilities on earth (Matt. 6:19 – 21). They will be surprised to find they have less treasure up there than they imagined, for those who have been negligent with worldly wealth will not be entrusted with true riches (Luke 16:11).

What might happen if Christians realized that everything they do matters to God? Consider the Great Recession. What if just the Christian home buyers had remained content to live within their means? What if just the Christian mortgage brokers had refused to offer subprime loans they knew the applicants could not afford? What if just the Christian financiers had refused to slice those toxic mortgages and repackage them to unsuspecting customers? If only those who claimed to follow Christ had lived as if he claimed their lives, the world might not have suffered the economic collapse we are still attempting to climb out of.

It's high time we broaden what it means to store up treasure in heaven. We store up treasure anytime we do something
God rewards. What does God
reward? Certainly he rewards

**THERE ARE NO**
**TIME-OUTS IN THE**
**CHRISTIAN LIFE.**

the obviously spiritual acts of
prayer, evangelism, and serving at
church. But he also rewards every
act of costly obedience, whether
that occurs in a boardroom, ball game, or grocery store. There
are no time-outs in the Christian life. It all counts now.

Do you love God? Then you can't love just him alone; you
must also love the people he has brought into your world. We will
learn what that means next.

# CHAPTER 10

# SERVE OTHERS

*We make a living by what we get, but we make a life by what we give.*

*Winston Churchill*

How can you tell if you're winning the game of life? The standard scoreboard looks something like this:

Success: What have you done?
Stuff: What do you have?
Status: What do other people think about you?

People kept score this way in the distant past, and it will be how they keep score far into the future. It applies both to East and West, men and women, the world and the church. People may count different things in various cultures and subcultures, but whether you're counting children, championships, sales, or souls saved, the same questions remain: How well did you do with whatever your people value, what do you have to show for it, and how well do others think you did?

They never stop counting until you're dead. Consider the sacred task of planting a church. The pastor may be focused on the noble goal of leading people to Jesus, making disciples, and expanding the body of Christ both numerically and spiritually. But someone — maybe even himself — will tally up the score. If after ten years the church is barely more than the handful of families he started with, he may conclude that he failed and try his hand at something else. He will feel even more pressure if the church he left takes off. No one wants to be remembered as the pastor who lost a once great church.

**THEY NEVER STOP COUNTING UNTIL YOU'RE DEAD.**

I feel some sympathy for megachurch pastors who shoulder the responsibility to lead their churches to new heights, bestselling authors who have to earn back their large advances, and A-list movie stars who are expected to beat back all comers on opening weekend. Each success inevitably generates more stress, as the next sermon, book, or movie will have even more at stake.

What if the way we keep score is not the way God keeps score? What if most people are kicking their ball at the wrong goal? Then it will happen, as Jesus said, that "many who are first will be last, and many who are last will be first" (Matt. 19:30).

These chapters on the meaning of life are a biblical peek at God's scoreboard. They answer the question by looking at what it means to be made in the image of God. Chapter 9 explained that our primary purpose is to know and love God, and before we leave the first page of Scripture, we learn a little more. Genesis 1:27 says:

So God created mankind in his own image,
in the image of God he created them;
male and female he created them.

Notice that the first two lines say the same thing, in reverse order, while the last one replaces the term "image" with an explanatory tag. What does it mean to be made in the image of God? It means we are made "male and female." Why is that significant? Because of who God is.

## MADE FOR COMMUNITY

The doctrine of the Trinity — that God is a loving Father, his beloved Son, and the Spirit who unites them in his bond of love — is a Christian distinctive. It is also a huge advantage. If God were merely a single person, as Jews and Muslims believe, he would be entirely self-centered. How could such a God love? He would have existed from eternity past all by himself, with literally no one and nothing else around.

Why would this singular person create something else to exist? Perhaps he was lonely, a single God, nonsmoker, looking for companions to enjoy long walks in a garden that he would provide. This God would inevitably sound desperate, as he had been waiting an eternity in what amounts to solitary confinement. He would be too needy to ever love truly.

A singular divine person might also create to show off his glory. Perhaps he grew tired of appreciating his awesomeness and wanted someone else to adore him. This God would be just as needy as the lonely God, but with a need for respect rather than a need for love. His quest for glory might seem less desperate than the longing for love, but he would be equally dependent on creation to supply what he could not give to himself.

> IF GOD WERE MERELY A SINGLE PERSON, AS JEWS AND MUSLIMS BELIEVE, HE WOULD BE ENTIRELY SELF-CENTERED.

Only our triune God can be entirely satisfied within himself. Our God is one, meaning he has no competitors. The Shema declares, "Hear, O Israel: The LORD our God, the LORD is one" (Deut. 6:4). Our God is holy and high above us. He is on the back of beyond, and everything exists for his glory alone. Our God is equally three. If God were merely one, then we might think he was self-absorbed. It might even be a sin for him not to be selfish, seeing how he is the most valuable being in the universe.[1] But if God is eternally three, a community of self-giving lovers, then it isn't possible for him to be selfish.[2] God has always loved the other within the Godhead. His very essence is love (1 John 4:8).

Jesus described the bond of love that exists among the divine persons when he said the Father is in him and he is in the Father (John 17:21 – 23). This mutual indwelling of the divine persons, what theologians call *perichoresis* in Greek and *circumincession* in Latin, means that the Father, Son, and Spirit are more united than anything we can imagine. None of them thinks, wills, or acts independently of the others. The Father knows, chooses, feels, and acts *in* the Son and *in* the Spirit; the Son does the same *in* the Father and *in* the Spirit; and the Spirit likewise *in* the Father and *in* the Son.

The closest we ever come in this life to imitating this divine interpenetration is in the act of sex. There is a reason, beyond the physical, why ecstatic participants say they "tasted the divine" or felt they "were knocking on heaven's door." When a man and a woman join bodies, they inevitably unite their souls, and their oneness is a reflection of the God who made them in his image. This sexual activity requires both partners to be unreservedly committed to each other. Any sex outside of the ironclad covenant of marriage is bound to hurt, for the wounded partners have ravaged what it means to be made in the image of God. They have treated the climax of their human identity as if it — and they — is nothing special. How can this not leave a mark?

The perichoretic unity of God is also why, after our basic needs for food and shelter are met, all other needs are essentially relational. The scoreboard of life may include success and stuff, but both of these depend heavily on our status. What others think about our success often determines how we evaluate what we accomplished. Have you ever completed a project and found few people cared? Maybe you put together a 4,000-piece jigsaw puzzle, wrote a book, or won the Most Eligible Bachelor Award at your local Comic-Con. You may have excitedly shared your success with family and friends, but if they merely shrugged, you gathered that what you did was not terribly important.

Relationships are also essential for enjoying our stuff. I once spent a lonely couple of days on Italy's Amalfi Coast. Its hairpin turns and ancient villages clinging to the mountainside are achingly beautiful, but I didn't enjoy them because I was missing my family and yearning to go home. A fine restaurant on an Italian beach isn't much fun when you're dining alone. A Hawaiian luau is even worse. I once made the mistake of going to one by myself, and I spent the entire night trying to disappear into clumps of people. I was in paradise, and I couldn't enjoy it because I had no one to share it with.

> A POOR MAN SURROUNDED BY FRIENDS HAS WEALTH BEYOND MEASURE, WHILE A RICH MAN WITH NO ONE TO CALL IS PITIFULLY POOR.

The Grant Study attempted to define the good life by tracking the lives of nearly three hundred Harvard men. The study began in 1937, when the men were sophomores, and it followed them for more than seventy years through war, career, marriage, divorce, parenting, grandparenting, retirement, and old age. George Valliant directed the study for four decades, and when asked, "What have you learned from the Grant Study men?" he replied, "That the only thing that really matters in life are your relationships to other people."[3]

A poor man surrounded by friends has wealth beyond measure, while a rich man with no one to call is pitifully poor. Why? Because God is triune, and he made us in his image as relational beings.

## MADE TO SERVE

Consider what God's trinitarian relationships are like. God is a community of self-giving lovers, three persons who set aside what might be in their own interests to serve the others. Jesus' prayer in Gethsemane, "Not my will, but yours be done," was not a shock (Luke 22:42). The Father did not say, "Whoa! Where did that come from?" The Son had always submitted his will to the Father. And any parent knows that Gethsemane was even more excruciating for the Father. He put aside his own desire to protect his Son and forsook him instead, so that ultimately Jesus might become the exalted Redeemer of the world. Likewise, the Spirit does not do whatever he wants but gladly obeys both the Father and the Son (John 14:26; 15:26).

This way of love is the way to life. Nothing is more alive than our triune God, and Jesus invites us to participate in this community of love when he declares, "Whoever wants to be my disciple must deny themselves and take up their cross and follow me. For whoever wants to save their life will lose it, but whoever loses their life for me will find it" (Matt. 16:24–25). Jesus was not offering the Big Trade, telling us that if we want treasures in the next life, we must settle for being miserable in this one. He was giving us the recipe for life now. If you want to live, really live, then do what Jesus and the other members of the Godhead do: Deny yourself. Live for someone else. Take up your cross — because your selfish nature must die — and follow Christ.

> IF YOU WANT TO LIVE, REALLY LIVE, THEN DO WHAT JESUS AND THE OTHER MEMBERS OF THE GODHEAD DO: DENY YOURSELF.

It is counterintuitive to think that losing your life is the way to find it, but you already know it's true. Aren't your happiest days when you set aside your own plans to serve another? You shaved your head to join her battle against cancer, carried boxes and furniture from early morning until the last load was moved in, or drove three hours to surprise him on his birthday. Your gesture was extravagant and unnecessary, but you went to bed with a broad smile because on this day you lived like the self-giving God who created you in his image.

This insight helps us to answer the question of this book, "Can you serve Jesus and still enjoy your life?" Joy always comes as a by-product of something else. Aim straight for it and it will inevitably slip through your fingers. Have you ever awakened with the sole intent of spending an entire day doing whatever made you happy? You couldn't wait to get to the beach, stadium, or amusement park. Do you remember how disappointed you felt on the ride home? You had some good moments, but the day didn't thrill you as much as you expected. But if you did the same activity with others, even *for* others, you found that your joy exponentially increased.

> WE ONLY FIND OUR LIVES WHEN WE GIVE THEM AWAY.

Service is the greatest act humans can do, as it imitates the self-giving life of God. If Jesus is the most deserving recipient, then denying ourselves and serving Jesus is the most satisfying thing we can ever do. The road may not always be easy, but have you ever met anyone who regretted taking up their cross and following Jesus? I've never heard an older saint say, "You know what? I wish I had lived a little less committed to the Lord. If I had to do it over again, I would have been a bit more selfish with my time and money, especially when I was establishing my family and career. I would be better off if I had served Jesus less."

Do you know why you'll never hear this? Because God is a trinity of self-giving lovers, and he created us in his image. We only find our lives when we give them away.

## MADE GOOD

The Trinity is also essential for explaining a central point of this book: Creation is good. If God is not triune, then either he created to fill some need (for glory or love) or because something went wrong. If God is a singular person, then either creation solves his problem or it is his problem to be solved.

Theologian Michael Reeves explains that the various strains of Gnosticism agreed that God is The One.[4] The only thing that existed eternally was this singular God in his good, spiritual world. Then, somehow, something emanated from this One. As this thing separated from The One, it was seen to be obviously inferior. Only the spiritual One was good; everything else was bad. So The One vomited this other out of its presence, which explains how the physical world came to be. Someday The One will return and suck the universe back into its happy singularity, and everything will be One again.

Unlike Genesis, which says God created a good world that cataclysmically fell into evil, the Gnostics said creation is the result of a prior fall. The physical world only exists because something somewhere went wrong. Scripture says creation is what God came to fix. Gnosticism says creation is the problem that The One seeks to eliminate.

The Gnostics preference for The One led them to despise anything — the universe, bodies, even women — that dispersed The One. The Gnostics noticed that, just as the physical world emanated from the spiritual One, so Eve came from the side of Adam (Gen. 2:21 – 23). They concluded that Eve must be much worse than Adam, which is why the Gnostic *Gospel of Thomas* ends with Peter saying, "Let Mary leave us, for women are not worthy of life." The Gnostic Jesus replies, "I myself shall lead her in order to make her male, so that she too may become a living spirit resembling you males. For every woman who will make herself male will enter the kingdom of heaven."[5]

Start with a singular divine person and everything that is not him becomes a problem. But if the one God is eternally three persons, then the uniqueness of the other already exists within him. God has never been alone, and neither must the man whom he has made in his image (Gen. 2:18). God created us male and female because he is a relational being, a community of self-giving lovers who invite us to participate in the boundless life of God. He is not threatened by the presence of others. Just as he is eternally diverse, so he created distinct genders to enrich the unity that comes from joining unique things.

God delights in diversity. He created an entire world of remarkably different animals and ecosystems, far richer than anything we could have imagined. We will examine our responsibility to them next.

# CHAPTER 11

# CULTIVATE
# THE EARTH

God milks his cows by those farmers he has assigned to
that task.

*Martin Luther*

O ne morning as I drove into work, I listened to a sermon
by my favorite radio preacher. His text was Ephesians
6:5 – 8, which encourages slaves to obey their masters with sin-
cerity, "just as [they] would obey Christ." They must "serve
wholeheartedly, as if [they] were serving the Lord." The preacher
read the passage and then apologized to his congregation. He
said he had checked his sermon files and realized he had seldom if ever preached a message on work. Since most people
spend one-third of their lives on the job, this was a significant
oversight.

The preacher went on to give a stirring message about work.
He exegeted the passage, explaining the similarities and dif-
ferences between first-century slaves and twenty-first-century
employees, what it meant to serve our bosses "with respect and
fear," and what reward faithful workers might expect from the
Lord. But he didn't explain how Paul could say that our work

is service to Jesus. This liberating truth is the foundation for a Christian perspective on work, which I'll explain now.

## GOD'S FIRST COMMAND

Paul's companion letter to Ephesians is his epistle to the Colossians, and near the end of that book he wrote something similar. Paul encouraged slaves, "Whatever you do, work at it with all your heart, as working for the Lord, not for human masters, since you know that you will receive an inheritance from the Lord as a reward. It is the Lord Christ you are serving" (Col. 3:23 – 24).

How could Paul tell slaves that their hard work was actually service to Jesus? Two chapters earlier, Paul said that Jesus is the Creator: "For in him all things were created: things in heaven and on earth, visible and invisible, whether thrones or powers or rulers or authorities; all things have been created through him and for him" (Col. 1:16). If Jesus is the Creator, then he is the one who first commanded the human race to "be fruitful and increase in number; fill the earth and subdue it. Rule over the fish in the sea and the birds in the sky and over every living creature that moves on the ground" (Gen. 1:28).

This verse has five commands. The first three — "be fruitful," "increase in number," and "fill the earth" — are shared with birds and fish (Gen. 1:22), but the final two — "subdue" and "rule" — are reserved for humans alone. These verbs are a crucial, and perhaps the most important, part of what it means to be made in the image of God. Genesis was written in the ancient Near East, where kings were said to bear the image of God because they governed their realms on behalf of a distant deity. Genesis democratizes the image by declaring that every human bears the image of God, not just kings. God made us as the climax of creation to rule the world on his behalf, and we each are responsible to mediate the blessing of God to that slice of creation that lies within our influence. We represent God to each other, the animals, and the earth, and we will give an account for the God they see in us.[1]

God elaborated on this priestly responsibility when he "took the man and put him in the Garden of Eden to work it and take care of it" (Gen. 2:15). There is a tension within this double command. On the one hand, we must "take care of" or guard (*shâ-mar*) the garden, preserving its resources for future generations. But we must not turn the earth into a museum, for God also commands us to "work" the garden. The Hebrew term is *'âbad*, which shares the same root as the word for slave. We are to serve creation, cultivating its raw materials into an escalating advance of culture. If I were God, I would have been content to command Adam and Eve, "Here is a beautiful, pristine world. Please don't break anything!" God expects more from his image bearers, and he invited Adam and Eve to improve on his creation by taking it to a higher place.

We call the commands of Genesis 1:28 and 2:15 the "creation mandate" or "cultural mandate." These commands occur in Scripture's opening scene, before the fall, and they direct us to develop human culture. Culture is what you get whenever humans intersect with nature. This is obviously true for metals that we twist into trumpets and cotton that we weave into shirts, but it's also true about more advanced technology. Your gleaming smartphone might seem several steps removed from nature, but the CPU that runs it is made of sand. Even language, the highest achievement of human culture, uses nature's instruments, such as vocal chords, pencil lead, and trees for paper, to describe a culture's place in the world. The cold, hard world influences the development of language, which is why Eskimos have more than fifty words for snow, West Michigan has several terms to distinguish Calvinists, and Cleveland sports fans have many ways to describe a half century of losing ("the shot," "the drive," "the fumble," "the decision").

**YOUR JOB IS THE ONE PLACE WHERE YOU ARE PAID FOR YOUR CULTURAL CONTRIBUTION.**

Your job is the one place where you are paid for your cultural contribution. Someone thinks your efforts enhance the human endeavor, and they reward you with whatever they deem your work is worth (or perhaps can get away with). This is why Paul told slaves they were serving the Lord Jesus. Their cultural contributions enabled them and others to develop creation, and so they were obeying the first command that Jesus, who is the Creator of all, gave to the human race. They were not merely serving their masters, but the Lord himself.

## WHAT THE REFORMATION WAS ABOUT

This recovery of the spiritual value of ordinary work lies at the heart of the Reformation. If you are a Protestant, what follows applies directly to you. Plato's dualism — heaven is good, the earth is bad; souls are good, the body is bad — so influenced Western civilization that by the Middle Ages it had become the default position of the Roman Catholic Church. A normal human life might be okay, but a person who really wanted to please God should aim higher and become a monk, nun, or priest. Money was permissible, but a spiritual person would take the vow of poverty. Marriage was good, a sacrament even, but a holy man would take the vow of celibacy. The church developed a two-tiered level of Christianity that reflected Plato's divide: a heavenly life for aspiring saints and a mundane, earthly existence for everyone else.

Their pious asceticism inevitably led the religious elite to think they were contributing to their salvation. They could easily see they were more committed to Christ than normal folks, for they had cloistered themselves from physical pleasures in order to devote themselves to the spiritual life. Look at all they had given up so their unfettered soul could float to heaven and become one with God!

This focus on what they were doing logically led to legalism, because they could always do a little more, and whatever they did was never enough. If your goal is to transcend the material world, then you might discipline your body to survive on four hours of sleep and rice and beans. But you could always sleep less and give up the beans! Even then you won't entirely free your soul from its physical needs. As long as you are alive, you will sleep sometime and eat something. Any Christian who attempts to practice Plato's dualism eventually will go insane. Don't believe me? Let me tell you about Martin Luther.

Luther pursued the Platonic plan of salvation to its logical end because he was acutely aware of the depths of his sin. The only way he knew to make up for his failures was to aim higher and become a monk. But though he permanently damaged his health by fasting three days at a time and sleeping without a blanket, he realized he could never rise high enough to satisfy the infinite standards of a holy God. How could he, a sinful human, ever do enough? Luther confessed, "I was myself more than once driven to the very abyss of despair so that I wished I had never been created. Love God? I hated him!"[2]

Finally, after years of anguish and driving his confessor crazy with imaginary sins, Luther discovered his Reformation breakthrough while studying the first chapter of Romans. He read Paul's admonition that "the righteous will live by faith" (Rom. 1:17) and finally understood this not as a command to become righteous but as a promise that anyone who believes will be covered by Christ's righteousness: "He who through faith is righteous will live."[3] Luther said, "I felt myself to be reborn and to have gone through open doors into paradise. The whole of Scripture took on a new meaning, and whereas before the 'justice of God' had filled me with hate, now it became to me inexpressibly sweet in greater love. This passage of Paul became to me a gate to heaven."[4]

Luther immediately began preaching the virtues of faith and freedom. He emphasized faith, because now he understood that salvation was something we receive rather than achieve. Salvation begins when we confess we can never climb up to God but can only rest in the work of the God who came down to us. We can't do enough spiritual good to earn God's approval but can only accept his acceptance of us in Jesus.

Luther realized this free salvation frees us to be normal people. In his small but essential treatise *The Freedom of a Christian*, Luther said the righteousness that we receive from Christ liberates us to serve our neighbor. When he was a monk, Luther spent all of his time and energy trying to save his own soul. But now that he knew he was secure, he suddenly had a lot of time on his hands! He was free to serve his neighbor in whatever ways were needed, whether spiritually or physically. Luther served his neighbor by prayer and preaching the Word. He could also serve him by baking a meal, shingling a roof, or sweeping the street. He now understood that the physical world helps rather than hinders our salvation, for it supplies numerous opportunities to express our gratitude to God by serving our neighbor.[5]

Luther said the opportunities to serve neighbor vary by our individual callings, or vocations. Many Christians mistakenly suppose that only those in "full-time" ministry have a calling from God. Ask Roman Catholics about vocation and they will likely think you are asking about becoming a priest. Attend a Protestant ordination council and you will hear about the pastoral candidate's "call to ministry." This is right and necessary, yet why don't we also speak of God's calling for nonministry positions? Are not rank-and-file Christians equally called to motherhood, mechanical engineering, or McDonald's? This may sound trite, but if you have ever eaten at a Chick-fil-A restaurant, you know that even fast food can be a divine calling.

We will say more about vocation in chapter 13, but for now I want you to think hard about the calling you are paid to do. If your job is too valuable to put a price on, such as homemaker, count it too. Your current position may not be your dream job, and that's okay. For now, it is where God has placed you to provide for your family and serve your corner of creation.

Here's the question: How does your job serve your neighbor and develop culture? What does your job make possible? For instance, if you are an accountant, then you are responsible for your company's integrity. You must tell the truth about what the business can and cannot afford. If you are a janitor, then you are in charge of hospitality, providing a clean and safe environment so the others may focus on their roles. If you are in sales, then your job is to meet your customers' needs and find orders to keep the other workers employed. If you are a receptionist, then congratulations: you are the face of the company, the person responsible for a good first impression.

> WHEN YOU ARE DYING, WHAT IS IT THAT YOU WOULD WANT TO HAVE ACCOMPLISHED? WHY NOT WORK ON THAT TODAY?

You must also think larger and ask how your company contributes to the story of God. What product or service does it create; what does it make possible for the world? Should Christians submit a bid to build a casino, recruit students who already are drowning in debt, work in the subprime mortgage department of a Wall Street bank, provide technical support to Victoria's Secret, vigorously defend clients whom they know are guilty, or bake a wedding cake for a gay couple? Christians may disagree about the answers to these questions, but we must ask them. If it's true that we spend one-third of our life at work, then when it's all said and done, a big chunk of what our life meant is what we did for our jobs. When you are dying, what is it that you would want to have accomplished? Why not work on that today?

Every wholesome calling, from missionary to dishwasher to cement truck driver, is eligible to receive the Lord's reward. Whatever your hands find to do, do it well and with all your might. Do it for the Lord, out of obedience to the first command he ever gave you, and he will be the one you are serving. We're all full-time Christians now.

# CHAPTER 12

# REST EVERY SEVENTH DAY

> Sunday feels odd without church in the morning. It's the time in the week when we take our bearings, and if we miss it, we're just following our noses.
>
> *Garrison Keillor*

**C**an you serve Jesus and still enjoy your life?

This is the question that opened this book and which every chapter attempts to help answer. But even their best points fall short without the crucial insight of this chapter.

*Can you serve Jesus and still enjoy your life?*

This question asks whether it's possible to integrate our Christian responsibilities with our human desires. Can we live for the high purpose of redemption and still enjoy the normal pleasures of creation? The key that unlocks the answer may surprise you. It floored me.

***Can you serve Jesus and still enjoy your life?***

The answer seems impossible because of our limited resources. There isn't enough of us to go around. Time spent at the beach with family is time not used to tell others about Jesus. Money placed in the offering plate is money not available for next summer's vacation.

There is also the problem of trust. We fear that if we tell Jesus we'll go anywhere and do anything, he might just take us up on it. The cost could be big, as with missionaries who send their children to boarding school for months at a time. It might also be small but still more than we're willing to pay. I'm embarrassed to admit this, but when I was in seminary, I heard a pastor of a thriving church say their secret was Sunday afternoon prayer meetings. My first thought was how wonderful it would be to have this pastor's ministry. My second thought was, "But I'll miss the NFL!" God toppled my idol by moving my team to Baltimore, where it promptly won the Super Bowl. I learned the hard but necessary lesson that while sports are an excellent diversion from life, they must never get in the way of life. How foolish!

**THE KEY TO SOLVING BOTH PROBLEMS— LIMITED RESOURCES AND LACK OF TRUST— IS FOUND IN GOD'S SPECIAL DAY OF DELIGHT.**

The key to solving both problems — limited resources and lack of trust — is found in God's special day of delight. This chapter argues that Sabbath rest is essential for enjoying life, and only Christians are wholly able to keep it holy. If this is true, then not only is serving Jesus not a roadblock to enjoying life, but it is the only way we can.

## GIFT OF REST

The problem of limited resources assumes that creation and redemption must always compete. Attention paid directly to creation cannot simultaneously be paid to redemption, and vice versa. This is true so long as we focus on what we are *doing*, as we only have so much money and energy to spread around. But what if creation and redemption are reconciled at a deeper level, not by doing but by *not doing*? This is precisely what Scripture teaches about the Sabbath.

The Hebrew verbal root for Sabbath (*shâbat*) literally means "to cease or rest." Stop. Take a break. Don't do anything of economic or pragmatic value, on purpose. And the reason for this rest? Would you believe it's *both* creation and redemption?

Exodus 20:8 – 11 says we must rest every seventh day to follow God's example when he made the world: "For in six days the LORD made the heavens and the earth, the sea, and all that is in them, but he rested on the seventh day. Therefore the LORD blessed the Sabbath day and made it holy" (v. 11). Deuteronomy 5:12 – 15 also grounds the Sabbath rest in redemption. God tells Israel to rest every seventh day to celebrate their deliverance from slaving seven days a week in Egypt. "Remember that you were slaves in Egypt and that the LORD your God brought you out of there with a mighty hand and an outstretched arm. Therefore the LORD your God has commanded you to observe the Sabbath day" (v. 15).

To understand how the Sabbath integrates creation with redemption, we must learn what it means for each. The Sabbath was the climax of creation week, when God stepped back and savored the works of his hands. He blessed the Sabbath and said it was holy, a day to delight in the beauty of his world and enjoy leisurely communion with Adam (Gen. 2:2 – 3). God commands us to follow his example, to rest every seventh day to appreciate family, friends, and the life we have made. Rest is the goal of work, not the other way around. We don't rest merely so we can work, but we work so we can rest and enjoy what we have done.

Rest is not only our finish line. It's the starting line too. Creation week underscores the primacy of rest by starting humanity with a Sabbath. As a creature of the late sixth day, Adam's first full day on earth was the seventh-day rest. He took a break even before he started to work (a practice still followed by Michigan road crews). The first Sabbath was God's special gift. It wasn't a reward for a good week of work. Rather, it was the starting point for the week ahead.

Sabbath is a gift because it is a day for enjoyment. This day doesn't just permit us to take a break; it orders us to be nonproductive, to refuse to show up for work. To stop whatever it is we are doing and just be. To lift our eyes from the grindstone and see the bigger picture. To soak in the pleasure of being alive in this beautiful world that God made especially for us. We properly enjoy the Sabbath when we spend it on whatever rejuvenates us. When we invite friends over for lunch, take a nap or a walk in the woods, play tennis, or read just for fun. When we daydream about anything or nothing at all.

> THE FIRST
> SABBATH ...
> WASN'T A REWARD
> FOR A GOOD WEEK
> OF WORK. RATHER,
> IT WAS THE
> STARTING POINT
> FOR THE WEEK
> AHEAD.

Because the Sabbath is a gift, it won't force itself on us. Like any other gift, it must be received. This is harder than it sounds, because we won't accept and unwrap the Sabbath unless we are content. Only those who have enough are willing to rest with whatever they have. When we start our week with the Sabbath, we are saying our lives are already full. We don't work to fill a void or make a name for ourselves. We labor from gratitude, not to become somebody but because we are somebody. We already have enough, even before we accomplish anything.

## TEST OF FAITH

The Sabbath conveys this same liberating message in the realm of redemption. I must say right at the top that Christians aren't obligated to keep the Sabbath as Jews were in the Old Testament. The Sabbath is the only one of the Ten Commandments not reissued in the New Testament, and the reason given is because its day of rest has been fulfilled in Jesus (Col. 2:16 – 17). The children of Israel longed for the promised rest of Canaan, which as a type of Christ is now received by we who stop trying to earn our salvation and rest in Christ's finished work (Heb. 3:7 – 4:11).

If Jesus has provided our permanent rest, then we may either discard the Sabbath as something outdated or continue to keep it as a silent witness to our faith in Christ. No Christian should be forced to observe the Sabbath, for we are free in Christ to consider "one day more sacred than another" or to consider "every day alike" (Rom. 14:5). However, every Christian who neglects the Sabbath should at least stop and ask why that is. Is it because we are free in Christ? Fine. Is it because we don't think we can afford a break? Not fine.

Is our world so fragile that it might unravel if we aren't constantly on call? Are we afraid we will lose ground to colleagues who relentlessly work through the weekend? If these are our reasons, then working 24/7 indicates we trust something else besides Jesus. Jesus isn't really enough, but we'll only be satisfied when we achieve a bit more money, success, or something. We work nonstop, as if our salvation depended on us.

The Sabbath supplies a surprisingly accurate barometer of our spiritual health. Only those who trust entirely in Jesus are free to put the world in its place and take a break every seventh day. We won't observe the Sabbath in a legalistic way, fixated on what tasks we must not do, for this shifts the focus back onto us and implies that our standing with God depends on what we are able to deliver. But embracing the truth that we have been given fullness in Christ (Col. 2:10), we are free to be unproductive on purpose.

> IS OUR WORLD SO FRAGILE THAT IT MIGHT UNRAVEL IF WE AREN'T CONSTANTLY ON CALL?

And since the entire day is a silent testimony to the gospel, why not use the best part of it for corporate worship? The early Christians transposed the Sabbath into the Lord's Day, meeting on the first day of the week to celebrate the resurrection of their Lord. John Calvin thought it would be terrific if Christians could worship together every day, but since this is impractical, we should at least meet every week to hear God's Word and respond with songs and prayers. In a sermon on the Sabbath, Calvin said the Lord's Day is like a high tower that we climb in order to survey the terrain of our lives. We look back on the many ways God has graced us, which then fills us with gratitude that fuels the week ahead. Calvin said that if we're too busy to make time for this, then we are no better than brute beasts.[1]

## REST OF FAITH

How then does Sabbath keeping help to answer the question, "Can you serve Jesus and still enjoy your life?" It solves the problem of limited resources — will we have anything left for enjoying creation if we give everything for the sake of redemption? — because no resources are required. We only need resources when we aim to *do* something. But if we're merely trying to rest, then we can stop whatever we're doing and relax in the work that Christ has already done.

The Sabbath rest solves the problem of trust because it assures us that God is on our side. He doesn't demand our allegiance so that he can ruin our lives, but so that he can lead us to refreshment, contentment, and satisfaction. The God who delivers everlasting rest must have our best interests at heart. We can trust that he wants us to enjoy our lives to the full, both now and forever (John 10:10).

WE CAN TRUST THAT GOD WANTS US TO ENJOY OUR LIVES TO THE FULL, BOTH NOW AND FOREVER (JOHN 10:10).

But might not Sabbath keeping lull us into complacency? Might it become a spiritual excuse to be satisfied with earthly pleasures and ignore the lost people who are going to hell? How can we take a weekly time-out when the need is so great? I have four things to say in response, and because I am Baptist, I will alliterate them.

First, Sabbath keeping is an opportunity to *proclaim* the gospel. A Lord's Day that is centered on corporate worship provides ample opportunity for visitors to hear the gospel, and many have been brought to faith as they worship with us. Besides, non-Christians expect us to meet every Sunday, and they likely won't take us seriously if we aren't meeting regularly to worship God.

Second, Sabbath keeping helps to *preserve* the gospel. The Sabbath establishes a rhythm to life that burrows the gospel into our bones. When people ask what it means to rest in the promises of God and how they can tell whether they are doing it, why not invite them to share the Sabbath? Bring them to church, where the simple fact of our gathering bears witness to the gospel that may bring them to that ultimate day of rest.

Third, Sabbath keeping *purifies* our faith in the gospel. Our weekly break forces us to confront where our trust really lies. Do we have enough confidence in God to go to the bench, or do we somehow think the success of the gospel depends on us? William Willimon applies this to pastors, writing that "Sabbath keeping is a publicly enacted sign of our trust that God keeps the world, therefore we do not have to. God welcomes our labors, but our contributions to the world have their limits. If even God trusted creation enough to be confident that the world would continue while God rested, so should we."[2]

Fourth, Sabbath keeping *propels* us to share the gospel. The same faith in God that permits us to rest every Sabbath also empowers us to work hard the other six days. Imagine the hopelessness of the task if we thought that bringing others to Christ depended on us and how hard we worked! But if we trust God enough to knock off every seventh day, we may certainly trust him to draw sinners to himself. God's sovereignty shouldn't lead us to say, "Why bother? God is going to save whomever he wants." Rather, it inspires us to work harder because we know that God's power means our efforts have a good chance at success.

We will also work better because we will be laboring from gratitude. Our efforts will not be frantic attempts to make something important from our lives, but rather they will be our free and thankful response because we know the defining question of our lives is already settled. We won't tell others about Jesus in a futile effort to make our life count. We will share Christ precisely because it already does.

Can you serve Jesus and still enjoy your life? "Remember the Sabbath day by keeping it holy" (Ex. 20:8), and you'll see.

# CHAPTER 13

# WHAT IS YOUR CALL?

*The point is to love God and neighbor, and to take up the
cross in the self-sacrificial paths defined by one's callings.*
*Douglas Schuurman*

W e have learned that creation is good, is our home, and
contains the meaning of life. God has placed us on earth
to love him, serve others, responsibly develop culture, and rest
every seventh day. We honor God through worship, sports, gardening, and whatever we do, if we "do it all in the name of the
Lord Jesus, giving thanks to God the Father through him" (Col.
3:17). We Christians should thrive in our human lives.

But is this enough? In his bestselling book, *Radical*, David
Platt describes three people who seem to be winning at life: a university student diligently preparing for a career, a businessman
with a corner office and a large house in the suburbs, and a retired
couple contemplating how best to enjoy their golden years. Platt
writes, "Imagine these common scenarios and then ask the question, 'Were we created for something much greater than this?'"[1]

John Piper thinks so. In *Don't Waste Your Life*, he laments
the many people who think "the Christian life means simply

avoiding badness and providing for the family." These people work hard during the day, watch TV and PG-13 movies in the evening, avoid all major sins, and relax and go to church on the weekends. Piper says, "This is life for millions of people. Wasted life. We were created for more, far more." He explains: "No one will ever want to say to the Lord of the universe five minutes after death, I spent every night playing games and watching clean TV with my family because I loved them so much. I think the Lord will say, 'That did not make me look like a treasure in your town. You should have done something besides provide for yourself and your family.'"[2]

I understand what they are trying to say. We serve a big God, and we shouldn't settle for small ball if God has big plans for us. Perhaps we are too easily pleased. But I also fear loading hardworking Christians with false guilt. Paul commanded believers "to make it your ambition to lead a quiet life: You should mind your own business and work with your hands, just as we told you, so that your daily life may win the respect of outsiders and so that you will not be dependent on anybody" (1 Thess. 4:11 – 12). This sounds like Piper's description of a wasted life, yet Paul instructs Spirit-filled believers to aim for it.

What is the shape of a godly, valuable life? This is a nuanced question that deserves a nuanced analysis. Fortunately, the Corinthians raised this question, so we have God's answer.

## CONFUSED IN CORINTH

The Corinthians believed that singleness was good and marriage was bad because of their Platonic view of the world. This put Paul in an awkward spot because he agreed that singleness was better but not for the ungodly reason they gave. So Paul laced his argument in 1 Corinthians 7 with qualifiers, shelving his usual "Thus says the Lord" for the more hesitant "I have no command from the Lord, but I give a judgment as one who by the Lord's mercy is trustworthy" (v. 25).

Paul offered two reasons why it's better to remain single, as he was (1 Cor. 7:7). First, there was a "present crisis" in Corinth, perhaps a famine or hostile environment to Christianity that would cause additional trouble for those who were married (vv. 26 – 28). Like Peter Parker who fears that marrying Mary Jane will make him more vulnerable to the enemies of Spiderman, so those who have more attachments will suffer more when trouble comes.

Second, Paul said it is wise to remain single because "the time is short" (1 Cor. 7:29). We live in an emergency situation. The kingdom has broken into our world, and we do not know how much time we have left until Jesus returns. Those who "use the things of the world" must not become "engrossed in them. For this world in its present form is passing away" (v. 31). As the final minute of a basketball game has frequent time-outs, intentional fouls, and desperate heaves at the basket — something that would be out of place in the middle of the second quarter — so we who live in the last days may make choices that would seem strange in normal times.

Despite the advantages of being single, Paul repeatedly affirmed the goodness of marriage. It is not a sin to marry (1 Cor. 7:28, 36), because marriage is God's gift that he "created to be received with thanksgiving by those who believe and who know the truth" (1 Tim. 4:3). How does one decide whether to remain single or marry? Paul said it is wise to remain single if a person has the "gift" of celibacy (every hormonal teenager understands why that word belongs in quotation marks), but either way it doesn't matter (1 Cor. 7:7). Whether married or single, free or slave, every Christian "should live as a believer in whatever situation the Lord has assigned to them, just as God has called them" (v. 17).

How do you know what God wants from you? Look at your callings. Where has God placed you? Whom are you obligated to serve? Our most important callings arise from our covenantal relationships. I am called to be a husband, father, son, brother, and church member, and each of these callings is too valuable to receive a paycheck. I would be insulted if Avery or Landon slipped me $10 for being their dad or my pastor gave me a kick-back for inviting people to church. This will be essential to remember should you ever find yourself unemployed. You may not have a job at the moment, but your most valuable callings remain unchanged.

Beyond your covenantal relationships, examine where you are in the world. Your job as a restaurant server or sandwich artist may be a stepping-stone to something else, but as long as you hold that job, it is precisely what God has called you to do. Paul tells slaves not to fret that they are only slaves. They should take their freedom if they can get it, but it won't change their status before God. They are "the Lord's freed person," so they may con-tentedly "remain in the situation they were in when God called them" (1 Cor. 7:22 – 24).

> HOW DO YOU
> KNOW WHAT GOD
> WANTS FROM YOU?
> LOOK AT YOUR
> CALLINGS.

You are free in the Lord to change your paid job, and when you do, that new job becomes your new calling, the place where you can love God by serving neighbor and contributing to cul-ture. You can change callings because the pay is better, but the best moves tend to follow Frederick Buechner's advice: "The place God calls you to is the place where your deep gladness and the world's deep hunger meet."[3] What do you enjoy doing, and what does the world need? It's your call.

## HIGHER ISN'T BETTER

This may be controversial, but there does seem to be a sense in which some callings are higher than others. Paul argued that single people are free to give "undivided devotion to the Lord" while married people's "interests are divided" between the Lord and their spouse (1 Cor. 7:32 – 35). As the supernatural realm transcends the natural, so those who are privileged to devote the lion's share of their time to God are in a special position. In this sense, being called into Christian ministry is a uniquely high calling, or "noble task" (1 Tim. 3:1).[4]

And yet, in another more important sense, all wholesome callings are equal. God rewards our heart, not the height of our calling. Whatever you do, "whether in word or deed," do you "do it all in the name of the Lord Jesus, giving thanks to God the Father through him" (Col. 3:17)? Then you will receive your reward, and it will be much larger than that of the preacher who ministered the Word — an objectively high calling — for mere fame or money.

As both the human body and the church need all the different parts pulling together, so every wholesome calling is indispensable to the whole (1 Cor. 12). A pastor may wrongly think his calling makes him superior to snowplow drivers, but in the dead of winter he can't have church without them. A missionary may suspect she is serving God better than the ordinary members of her sending church, but she won't stay long on the field if they don't pay her way. Ordinary jobs are the foundation of any society. As we learned in the Great Recession, when we lose jobs, we lose communities, and when we lose communities, we lose schools, parks, and churches. We can't have a church without normal jobs to support it.

Larry Osborne tells how a highly gifted pastor lost his job because he had an affair. Not long after, another pastor offered him a teaching position at his church, and when he explained the hire to his congregation, the pastor said, "This man is simply too gifted to waste his time selling shoes."[5] Ouch! Imagine how every salesclerk in his church must have felt! I have three brothers, all of whom work in business. One Christian intended to compliment my parents when he said, "You must be grateful that one of your sons is doing something of eternal significance!" Ouch again! Isn't there eternal significance in showing up for work each day?

Martin Luther explained why higher callings aren't necessarily better:

God cannot bear to see anyone neglect the duties of his calling or station in life in order to imitate the works of the saints. If therefore a married woman were to follow Anna in this respect, leave her husband and children, her home and parents in order to go on a pilgrimage, to pray, fast and go to church, she would do nothing else but tempt God, confound the matrimonial estate with the state of widowhood, desert her own calling and do works belonging to others. This would be as much as walking on one's ears, putting a veil over one's feet and a boot on one's head, and turning all things upside down. Good works should be done, and you ought to pray and fast, but you must not thereby be kept from or neglect the duties of your calling and station.[6]

Godly mothers must take Luther's words to heart. I met a homeschooling mom who feels guilty when a frantic morning squeezes out her quiet time with God. I told her it's good that she desires to read her Bible and pray, but an occasional miss is not something to worry about. "You kept seven children alive," I said, "and you educated them too! If you did this calling for the Lord, then you still served God, even on those days when you missed your devotions."

I know of a pastor who neglects his wife and daughters to spend time alone with God. When confronted, he appeals to 1 Corinthians 7, "From now on those who have wives should live as if they do not.... For this world in its present form is passing away" (vv. 29 – 31). If he carefully read the entire chapter, he would realize that his time spent with God is disobedience to God, because he has abandoned what God has called him to. It's a sin to live with a single person's "undivided devotion to the Lord" (v. 35) when you're married with children. This pastor piously dismissed his daughters' need for a loving father, and now their husbands must sort through the wreckage.

I know of another pastor who entered the ministry because it seemed like the most important thing he could do. The problem is, he isn't very good at it. The stress of preaching twice each week when he lacks the gift of teaching is more than he can bear. He looks twenty years older than he actually is, and he'll likely die before his time. I wish someone he trusts could put his arm around him and say, "You don't have to do this. You're free in Christ to do something you enjoy, something you're good at. You don't need to kill yourself doing someone else's calling."

Of course, as long as he stays in his current role, being a pastor is his calling. He should pray for strength and do his best, knowing that he will receive his reward. But his reward might be even greater if he changes to a job that is better suited to his gifts and interests. God needs pastors, but he also needs florists, bus drivers, and middle managers.

What is God calling you to do? It may be radical or it might be normal. But whatever it is, it's definitely spiritual. "Always give yourselves fully to the work of the Lord, because you know that your labor in the Lord is not in vain" (1 Cor. 15:58).

# PART 3

# FALL

Our tension between serving Jesus and enjoying life rises from Adam's fall. In an unfallen world, there would be no need for redemption, so the tension between creation and redemption would be eliminated. In an unfallen world, there would be no death, so we wouldn't be troubled by the tension between the natural and supernatural realms. We would have all the time in the world to worship God and enjoy the pleasures of creation. Finitude only bothers us because of the fall.

In an unfallen world, we would not play the natural and the supernatural against each other, neglecting God for the world or the world for God. The latter may seem pious, but it ultimately folds us into God and destroys the possibility of loving him. In an unfallen world, serving Jesus and having joy wouldn't seem mutually exclusive, because we would eagerly follow the trinitarian pattern and find our lives by losing them.

But we don't. Adam's fall ruined everything, and its damage divides and spreads faster than the embryonic stem cells of rabbits. The carnage of the fall litters every corner of creation. We stumble across it in our jobs, churches, families, and even our own hearts. This is a terrible problem — and an opportunity. Heroes are forged in the fires of tragedy. You cannot win a Purple Heart without the presence of war, rescue a drowning child unless she is sinking, or adopt an orphan unless his life has already gone terribly wrong.

This introduction must end, but it's not finished. Closure isn't possible until Jesus returns. Don't try to make sense of sin — that gives it too much credit — but patiently hope for the day of redemption.

# CHAPTER 14

# THE FALL THEN AND NOW

The heart wants what it wants.

*Woody Allen*

I didn't realize how windy it was around our house until I installed a storm door. Invariably someone would forget to latch it shut and the wind would catch the door, blowing it back and forth until the brackets pulled out of the jamb. I fixed the door several times, dutifully filling the reamed holes with broken chopsticks, drilling new holes, and tightening the brackets with longer and more menacing screws. Each fix proved more difficult than the last, and I began to worry that pretty soon I might need to replace the jamb.

So I called my family together for a Come to Jesus meeting. "We have to make sure we close the door until it latches," I began, "because I won't be able to fix it forever. I've begged you to shut it all the way and you still won't, and I don't know what else I can do. You know, maybe storm doors aren't meant for us. You'd think we'd be able to have one — other families do — but maybe the responsibility is too great. Maybe Wittmers aren't supposed to have storm doors. I'd like to keep it because it's nice to roll down the screen and let the breeze blow in, but if it breaks again that may be the end. I'll take the door off and we'll just be hot." I went around the room and made each person promise to shut the door until it latched and to make sure that any friend they were with did the same. We are all responsible for the door!

A week later I was in my upstairs office when I heard the metallic *whip-whap* of the storm door blowing back and forth. I ran downstairs, and sure enough, the bracket screws had popped out of the jamb. I saw that my wife was giving piano lessons in the next room, so I enthusiastically confronted her on the spot. How could she let this happen? The very thing we had just talked about and promised to do better!

She said it wasn't her fault. One of her students had left without latching the door. "So it is your fault," I replied. "You're responsible for your students, remember?" She said she couldn't have walked her out because she had already started a lesson with a new student. "But you have to! At least if you want to keep the door!" Back and forth we went, later that night and into the next day, my wife saying she couldn't be in two places at once and me saying she had to be more responsible. The issue was finally resolved when my neighbor came over and found the problem. Apparently I had put the brackets into the jamb backward.

THE SIN THAT RAVAGED THE HUMAN RACE SUPPLIES THE TEMPLATE FOR EVERY SIN SINCE.

I know what you're probably thinking, but I still think I had a point. And do you know why? Because of the fall. The sin that ravaged the human race supplies the template for every sin since. Adam's fall didn't just happen way back when; it still happens. We imitate his rebellion every day.

# THE FALL HAPPENED

An increasing number of Christians are denying there was a historical Adam who brought sin and death into the world — which means they can explain neither. Langdon Gilkey was Reinhold Neibuhr's teaching assistant, and he knew personally many of the mainstream theologians of the twentieth century. He said none of them believed that Adam's fall actually happened, so none could explain the problem of sin or why death is a problem.[1]

1. *The problem of sin.* Gilkey said his friends took Adam's fall as a symbolic story about the origin of sin. But if Adam is merely a symbol, then his story cannot explain "why each of us, and all of us together, fall." Gilkey explained, "A symbol at best *discloses* our situation to us; it does not provide for us an *explanation* of what the symbol discloses."[2] If Adam was not a real person whose rebellion corrupted his descendants, then why does every human sin as soon as he or she is able?

The cause cannot be merely our environment. A mother may coddle her child from birth through the terrible twos, catering to his every whim and cry, yet the first word he will master, and repeat often, is a defiant *No!* The Christian teaching that our children are born corrupted with Adam's sin may not be popular, but as G. K. Chesterton said, it is the "only part of Christian theology which can be really proved."[3] Every parent knows it's true. I didn't teach my kids to scratch and scream; they came that way. They inherited their sin nature from me, just as I inherited it from my parents, who got it from their parents, all the way back to Adam. No other explanation can account for the universality of sin.[4]

2. *Why death is a problem.* Gilkey observed that if there is no historical fall, then death must be a normal part of creation.[5] The scientific theory of evolution suggests that life on earth advances through natural selection and the survival of the fittest, both of which require death. Death is necessary to thin the herd and pass on the strongest genes to the next generation. Death is a natural part of life, and maybe its most important. As Steve Jobs told

Stanford graduates, "Death is very likely the single best invention of Life. It is Life's change agent. It clears out the old to make way for the new. Right now the new is you, but someday not too long from now, you will gradually become the old and be cleared away."[6]

Modern science may teach that even human death is good, but deep down everyone knows better. I doubt Jobs's own words offered him much comfort when he lay dying of pancreatic cancer. What if someone had said, "Sure, this stinks for you, but think of the young person who is now going to get your job and provide for his family. See, it's all good!"

I appreciate the honesty of New Atheist Victor Stenger, who admits he is terrified to face the nothingness of death. He would much rather believe that he will live forever with God, but he thinks science has proven he is nothing more than a collection of atoms that will disperse when he dies. All that is left is to enjoy his wife and children now, though he knows ultimately it won't matter anyway. He writes, "It is going to be very difficult for me to practice what I preach," but he encourages his fellow atheists to die with "a state of mind where the self does not matter and nothingness is approached with peace of mind."[7] Tragically, fading out of existence is his best-case scenario.

Christians face increasing pressure to deny a historical Adam and his cataclysmic fall, but we won't understand our greatest enemies without them. The next chapter will examine what the fall teaches us about death. Here is what we learn about sin.[8]

## ORIGINAL SIN

God created a fertile garden of delight and told Adam to enjoy the fruit from every tree except one. He and his wife "must not eat from the tree of the knowledge of good and evil, for when you eat from it you will certainly die" (Gen. 2:17). The serpent came along and gave a decidedly different interpretation of the tree. He directly contradicted God's word. "'You will not certainly die,' the serpent said to the woman. 'For God knows that when you eat from it your eyes will be opened, and you will be like God, knowing good and evil'" (Gen. 3:4 – 5).

Eve should have picked up a stick and bashed in the serpent's brains. How dare he insinuate that the Giver of life and every good thing did not have her best interests at heart! What had the snake ever done for her? But rather than promptly and joyfully

> EVE SINNED IN HER HEART BEFORE SHE SINNED WITH HER HAND. HER SIN WAS AUTONOMY.

submit to her Creator, Eve elevated herself above both God and the serpent. She appointed herself as judge. She would decide who was telling the truth. She used her God-given empirical and rational skills to put God on trial. Eve "saw that the fruit of the tree was good for food and pleasing to the eye, and also desirable for gaining wisdom," so "she took some and ate it" (Gen. 3:6).

Eve sinned in her heart before she sinned with her hand. Her sin was autonomy, a technical term that comes from two Greek words: *nomos*, which means "law," and *auto*, which means "car." Actually "auto" means "self," which is where we get our term for car. An automobile is a car you drive by yourself. (Whoever came up with that name obviously wasn't married!) Autonomy means "self-law." Rather than submit to God's command, Eve became a law unto herself. She decided to do whatever seemed right to her. If that happened to coincide with what God said, all the better. But if not, then too bad for God.

> I NEVER SIN FROM IGNORANCE. I KNOW WHAT GOD WANTS FROM ME, BUT TOO OFTEN I JUST DON'T CARE.

Adam's sin was even more inexcusable. He saw the shadow of shame and fear fall over Eve's face, heard the panic in her voice, and ate with the full knowledge of the consequences. Adam acted foolishly because he acted autonomously. He wanted to do whatever he wanted to do, just because he wanted to do it. No one, not even God, would be allowed to cramp his style.

As the head of the human race, Adam passed his twisted will down to each of us, who sin whenever we act autonomously. I never sin from ignorance. I know what God wants from me, but too often I just don't care. I want to do what I want to do just because I want to do it. I don't want anyone, especially God, telling me what to do.

## THE FALL HAPPENS

Autonomy is the reason I fought my family over the storm door. And to be fair, it is also the reason they rolled their eyes at me. The serpent was right when he said that eating from the forbidden tree would give knowledge of good and evil, but now we fight over what goes in which category. What is good for me may not be good for you, so we go to war to get our way.

Every war that has ever been fought began without a first shot. No one ever says they started it. They are just trying to protect themselves or correct an injustice that happened to them. Currently America is trying to stop Iran from developing nuclear weapons. Iran says their nuclear program is peaceful, but they probably think they need nuclear weapons to defend themselves against Israel, who already has them. Israel says they need nuclear weapons to defend themselves against the neighboring Arabs, who are angry that their land was taken away and given to a reconstituted Israel. Israel received the land as partial restitution for enduring the Holocaust, which Hitler conducted in order to liberate the Aryan race, which he claimed had been polluted by Jews.

Do you see why God told Adam not to eat from the forbidden tree? Autonomous people are sure that everyone else is ripping them off. And because everyone else is also autonomous, they are probably right. The rich hate the poor who pay no income tax but receive lots of free money and services. The poor hate the wealthy One Percenters who lobby their representatives and hide money in offshore accounts. White people think people of color imagine racism where it doesn't exist, while people of color think white people don't appreciate how many ways society favors them. Factory workers suspect their soft-handed managers are overpaid, while the bosses wish their grunts would work harder. Each thinks the other is getting too much, and each has a point.

Autonomy is the reason no one wants to admit they're wrong, even when they are caught red-handed. Ariel Castro was sentenced to life in prison plus one thousand years for kidnapping and torturing three teenage girls over eleven years. He defiantly told the court, "I'm not a monster. I'm sick." He claimed he was "a good person" who had been abused as a child and now simply was addicted to sex and pornography. In his mind, he and his chained victims enjoyed a happy home with lots of "harmony."[9]

Lesser sinners adopt a similar strategy. One woman who admitted to multiple affairs sought refuge in autonomy when she said, "I just need to learn to forgive myself." No, what you need is the forgiveness of God. You don't get to play the victim, the hero in your own story. You are not the one who offers forgiveness, not even to yourself. No part of you is innocent. You are nothing but the perpetrator, the one who is entirely in the wrong. Unless you admit that, you will not be able to receive the forgiveness you desperately need from God and those you have sinned against.

Autonomy is the reason we will never stop fighting the fall. There is no church, no family, no person who is not deeply ravaged by sin. Consider a philanthropic foundation that has pledged billions of dollars to end polio, malaria, and tuberculosis in sub-Saharan Africa. What could be more altruistic? And yet that foundation will have layers of bureaucracy that may become riddled with waste, greed, and mismanagement. Even if the foundation is mostly clean and efficient, it must still contend with corruption in the countries it seeks to help. A certain, and probably large, percentage of its grant will not make it to the field. And the aid that does get through may create new problems, such as overdependence on outsiders and power struggles over who controls and dispenses the vaccinations.

You may love your pastor and your healthy, growing church. Yet because it is staffed with sinners, there will always be sin to fight. Show up during the week rather than on performance Sundays, when we put our best foot forward, and you will see what I mean. You may have a beautiful and loving family, but you are always one slight or misunderstanding away from trouble. If you are honest, you know that the line between good and evil runs right through your own heart.

Your corner of the world may seem like Disneyland. It might even be Disneyland. But the "happiest place on earth" is still full of smiling sinners, so there will always be a need for Jesus. The next two chapters explain why.

# CHAPTER 15

# THE FALLOUT FROM THE FALL

[The world is] not the way it's supposed to be.

*Cornelius Plantinga Jr.*

I told my class of mostly urban, African-American pastors that our hope for the return of Christ and the resurrection of our bodies should influence how we conduct Christian funerals. We should celebrate the life of our deceased loved one, but we must also mourn her passing and remind the saints that she is not gone for good. At any moment, Jesus will return and resurrect her body, and she will live forever with him and us on this new, restored earth.

The pastors said they agreed with this, but they would get in trouble if they said it. The history of slavery and the continuing challenges of urban life have conditioned their people to think of death as a welcome deliverance from this vale of tears. Death is their happy homegoing to heaven. Why would they want to come back here?

## KNOW YOUR ENEMY

David Platt expresses a similar view of death in his book, *Radical*. He argues that *"the key* to taking back your faith from the American dream" is to "see death as reward." He writes, "The key is realizing — and believing — that this world is not your home." We "must focus our lives on another world," which we are privileged to enter the moment we die. He illustrates this point with a young college graduate who told her friends that while she could "get married and become a music teacher," what she really wanted was "to change my world" by traveling to the Middle East "to tell others about Jesus."

I applaud her choice to become a missionary, though her comment does seem to reflect the grandiose dreams of youth ("I want to change my world!") and appears too dismissive of wives and music teachers. Didn't she see the movie *Mr. Holland's Opus*? Still, I wish we had more devoted Christians like her. I felt her loss when Platt said she was killed in a bus accident in Egypt. Platt said her death was "not a story of tragedy but a story of reward," because she immediately "was ushered into the presence of Christ," where she will bask in his glory forever.[1]

I praise God that this young woman is now receiving her everlasting reward, but this does not mean her death was not also a tragedy. Paul said, "To die is gain," for he longed "to depart and be with Christ, which is better by far" (Phil. 1:21 – 23). But in the very next chapter, he mentioned Epaphroditus, who "was ill, and almost died. But God had mercy on him, and not on him only but also on me, to spare me sorrow upon sorrow" (Phil. 2:27). If God showed mercy to Epaphroditus by sparing his life, then death must be a bad thing.

Scripture says death is the first enemy that appears in human history. Its specter shows up before the Devil, when God warned Adam he would die if he ate from the forbidden tree (Gen. 2:17). Death is also our last enemy, hurled into the lake of fire four verses after the Devil is thrown in (Rev. 20:10 – 14). Scripture says

God can bring good things out of death, but nowhere does it call death a good thing. Paul was glad that death would bring him to Jesus, but he also called death "the last enemy" that Jesus came to destroy (1 Cor. 15:26).

Death is the reason you are a Christian. Have you noticed? Every religion exists to solve some problem. Buddhism tries to solve the problem of suffering, Hinduism seeks to overcome bad karma, and Islam attempts to fix the problem of pride. What problem does the Christian faith solve?

> IF YOU ARE NOT TROUBLED BY DEATH ... THERE IS NO CHANCE YOU WILL EVER PUT YOUR FAITH IN JESUS.

Sin and death. If you are not troubled by death, if the thought of being cremated or rotting in the ground does not scare and sicken you, there is no chance you will ever put your faith in Jesus. Why would you? He came to solve a problem you don't care about.

If we minimize death, saying it is our great reward, then we also minimize the victory of Christ that conquers it. Winning coaches always praise the losing team in their postgame press conferences. You will never hear a happy coach say, "Of course we expected to win. That other team is dreadful. They do not belong in our league." The winning coach always compliments the losing team, in part because the more he pumps them up, the better his team looks for beating them. Death doesn't need puffing. Everyone knows it is the dominant destroyer that one day will lay us out flat and cold. Let's not deny the obvious, but make much of death so we can make much of Christ. If we insist death is no big deal, then neither is the Jesus who defeated it for us.[2]

## UNDERSTAND YOUR ENEMY

Death is *the* consequence of Adam's fall. Adam and Eve did not immediately drop dead on the day they disobeyed, but they did die spiritually and did begin to die physically.[3] Adam and Eve hid from God, who is life itself (John 17:3). Their children turned to idols, prostituting themselves to any god who promised significance and security. Rather than serve their neighbor, Adam and Eve manipulated and blamed each other to get their own way. Soon one of their sons killed his brother, then Lamech murdered a man for merely wounding him (Gen. 4:8 – 11, 23 – 24). And rather than joyfully till the garden, Adam and Eve were exiled from Eden to hack stubborn thorns until they eventually died and returned to the soil.

In this way, death ravaged all three of our created relationships: We are sinners who are inclined to serve idols rather than the living God, to serve ourselves rather than our neighbors, and to work lazily for a paycheck rather than to responsibly cultivate the earth. Our sin dehumanizes us, hollowing us into shells of what we were intended to be. It also devastates the rest of creation. We bear the image of God and were placed here to rule this world on his behalf. So when we rebelled against our head, we took the entire planet down with us.

Like a stone tossed onto a pond, the fallout of the fall ripples out until it has corroded every corner of creation (Rom. 8:19 – 22). Animals who were given "every green plant for food" and one day will graze nonchalantly together are now prone to attack and eat each other (Gen. 1:30; Isa. 65:25). Even the ground is cursed, sprouting more weeds and disease than the vegetable plants we are trying to grow (Gen. 3:17 – 18). I love strawberries, blueberries, and peaches, but I have only ever eaten fruit from cursed soil. Imagine the flavors that will burst forth on the new earth! How sweet will orange juice taste when the curse is reversed! How blue will be the sea and sky, how green and lush our lawns, how melodious the music performed by birds, bullfrogs, and crickets!

But now we wait for Jesus' return, surrounded by the ravages of sin, knowing that it's our fault. Every time we sin, we vote for the death it brings. Every time we sin, we build the case against ourselves. Sinners like us don't merely deserve to physically die;

we deserve to suffer forever in hell. This is increasingly counter-cultural to say, as more and more Christians are questioning the reality of hell. But let's take a closer look at that. Is hell deserved? Or is it just something the church has made up to scare people into believing?

If we do not deserve hell, it's impossible to say why Jesus died. He could not have died to bear the hell we had coming, for we weren't headed there anyway. All we can say, at that point, is that the cross was a magnanimous display of love. But if that is all the cross was, it wasn't even that. Love is only love when it does something. If I rescue my wife from a raging river, people will call me a hero. I might even make the papers. But if my wife is standing beside me on the bank, and I say, "Look how much I love you!" and jump into the river, I'm just an idiot. I might still make the papers, but in the stupid column of the obituaries.

> SINNERS LIKE US DON'T MERELY DESERVE TO PHYSICALLY DIE; WE DESERVE TO SUFFER FOREVER IN HELL.

The cross is only an act of love if it truly rescues us from the hell we deserve. Minimize hell by saying that a loving and righteous God would never send us there, and we will be unable to explain why Jesus came. We might think his coming was nice, a gesture of goodwill, but we can't say it was necessary — which means it wasn't even nice. If the cross isn't necessary for our salvation, then the Father is wicked for making his Son go through with it.

The good news is that Jesus did come, to "fulfill all righteousness" as Israel's Messiah (Matt. 3:15) and to pay for our sin by his death and resurrection. And Jesus is coming again, to "punish those who do not know God ... with everlasting destruction" and to reign with his saints on this restored earth (2 Thess. 1:8 – 9; Rev. 21:1 – 7). That last part may not sound appealing to you. Perhaps you had a miserable time this go around, and the thought

of returning to earth leaves you cold. Stop and consider everything you do not like about your life. I guarantee every bit of it
is directly traceable to the fall. When sin and its devastation are
removed from the earth, you will flat out love it here.

I told my urban class that I understood why someone who has
endured a hardscrabble life would think of heaven as the ultimate
relief and would not want to come back. I also realize that as a
privileged white man I cannot begin to understand the suffering
of my urban friends. But I would humbly say that the return of
Christ and our reign with him should be especially meaningful
to them. They need to know they are not gone from this earth
for good when they die. The Christian hope is not merely that we
get to leave this painful life behind, closing our earthly chapter
and moving on to heaven. The promise of God is much better
than that. We may have left this earth on the bottom, but we are
coming back to reign with Christ. The very spot that brought so
much pain will be our place of greatest triumph. We will get over,
here on earth, where we were always meant to thrive.

This firm and certain hope inspires us to long for the return
of Christ and to pray the closing words of Scripture, "Come,
Lord Jesus" (Rev. 22:20). In the meantime, his imminent return
encourages us to fight the fall wherever we find it. May Jesus
catch us in the act when he comes again.

# CHAPTER 16

# HOW DO YOU FIGHT THE FALL?

You and I have need of the strongest spell that can be found
to wake us from the evil enchantment of worldliness.

*C. S. Lewis*

Some time ago a Baptist pastor asked my advice. He said one of the adult classes in his church wanted to hold a square dance. It seemed innocent enough, but it might also send the wrong message, since historically Baptists have opposed premarital sex on the grounds that it might lead to dancing. I wished him luck and said I was just a seminary student who happily didn't have to make such calls.

Today, in view of the Bible's unified story of creation, fall, and redemption, I could give him a much better answer. I would tell him to take out a sheet of paper and write two headings, Creation and Fall. Underneath Creation list the many goods that come with a square dance. It provides an opportunity for camaraderie, music, food, and old-fashioned fun. We might come up with a fairly long list. Underneath Fall write all the sinful aspects of a square dance. Not much comes to mind, unless someone brings a banjo. If our Creation category far outweighs the Fall, and if whatever we put under the Fall can be easily corrected (for example, we warn the senior saints to keep both feet on the floor), then we would conclude that a square dance is something we may do. (Notice that *may* does not imply *can*. Just because Baptists are allowed to dance doesn't mean we are able to do it well, especially since we don't drink alcohol, the very thing we need to loosen up.)

## WHERE THE FALL FINDS YOU

This creation/fall paradigm is useful for sorting out many knotty issues. I once attended a Christian athletics summit where a professor from a Big Ten school said he thought there might be something inherently wrong with competition. (This may say all you need to know about the sorry state of Big Ten football.) The professor said that when we compete, we are trying to beat the other team, put them at a disadvantage, trick them, and hit the ball where they can't reach it. None of these sound like what kind and loving Christians should do.

We addressed his concern by writing Creation and Fall on a whiteboard and filling up the Creation side with more than twenty goods of competition. It can be fun: Would you want to live in a world where you couldn't say to a friend, "C'mon, let's race"? Competition also provides a way to stay fit, improve our skills, connect with others, and so on. There were some significant problems too, such as cheating, disrespecting opponents, and thinking that winning was the only thing. But these fallen aspects supplied an opportunity for Christians to showcase the beauty of redemption. We could fix these errors and show the world what a difference Jesus makes in our sporting lives. So yes, Christians should compete, or they miss a promising advertisement for the gospel.

For another example, consider going to the movies. Some Christians refuse to watch a movie if it contains gratuitous sex, violence, and profanity, while others might praise its powerful story, honest dialogue, and fearless acting. We may disagree about whether we should see the movie, and the creation/fall model explains why. One person thinks there is enough creational good to merit wading through the smut, while another says the smothering presence of sin means it is not worth the risk.

> THESE FALLEN ASPECTS SUPPLIED AN OPPORTUNITY FOR CHRISTIANS TO SHOWCASE THE BEAUTY OF REDEMPTION.

Each film must be evaluated on its own merits, but it's worth saying that many Christians could use much more discernment. When I was in college, students were not allowed to go to movies, though we could rent them six months later from a video store. We knew the rule was hypocritical — why was it okay to watch a film in our living room but not in a theater? — and now, praise God, students are free to go to the cinema. The pendulum is always swinging, and now many Christians happily recommend movies that would have made their parents blush. They think they can see anything as long as they practice "discernment," which is code for watch whatever you want, regardless how raunchy, as long as you look for a Christ figure, a character yearning for redemption, or an illustration you can slip into your hip sermon.

Here's the problem. Christians claim to be on the side of redemption, so what business do we have of entertaining ourselves with the fall? Why would we ever want to celebrate sin? Sin is *the* problem. Sin is why Jesus died, and it is why you and I will eventually die. Sin will one day rob us of everyone and everything we have ever loved. We will die alone, and then they will bury us in the ground, where we will slowly decay. Hope you liked the movie.

The creation/fall model not only enables us to evaluate cultural products and activities, but it also suggests a method for staying pure. Evil is like rust on a car; it cannot exist on its own but always corrupts a prior good. The higher the good, the uglier it becomes when it turns evil. Lucifer is the Devil because originally he was the highest creature God ever made. If Lucifer was short, dumpy, and bald, he could only become TV comedian George Costanza — annoying but definitely not intimidating. But because Lucifer was a spectacular angel, when he went bad he became the Devil.

> EVIL IS LIKE RUST ON A CAR; IT CANNOT EXIST ON ITS OWN BUT ALWAYS CORRUPTS A PRIOR GOOD.

Likewise, the most heinous sins are terrible precisely because they pervert an extremely high good. Incest is the perversion of a father's love for his daughter. When this vital love goes bad, you shudder even to think of it. Pornography is the parody of sex, adultery is the perversion of marriage, cheating is the distortion of competition, and greed is the abuse of wealth.

When you are struggling with serious sin, remember that this sin is strong precisely because it is the perversion of an exceptionally powerful good of creation. So focus on that good. For example, it won't help someone who is addicted to pornography to repeatedly tell themselves to stop surfing for porn. The more they remind themselves not to look at porn, the more they will long for it. They would be much further ahead if instead they focused on the creational good of sex. How can they, in their present situation, appropriately enjoy God's gift of sex? Focus on that, and pornography's pull will seem much less powerful. Why settle for an empty perversion when you can have the real thing?

## WHERE YOU FIND THE FALL

The creation/fall paradigm is necessary for handling problems that come our way in the normal flow of life. We will watch something, play something, and eat and drink something, and this model enables us to sort out which things we should do and how we should do them. But committed Christians wonder whether it is enough to think redemptively only about the problems that find us. Shouldn't Christians also leave the comfort of their homes and churches and go out into the world to find problems to solve? Isn't it selfish to focus on our own circles, only sharing the gospel and acting redemptively toward others when the opportunity arises? Shouldn't we take the initiative and force the issue, proactively taking the light of Jesus into our dark and dying world?

This noble desire to make a difference for Jesus has prompted many Christians to adopt orphans from the other side of the world, start evangelistic conversations with strangers, take missions trips that bring Bibles and urgent medical care, and sponsor an impoverished child, family, or missionary who is serving among them. These acts of sacrificial love are worthy of high praise, and the need is overwhelming. But no individual or church can adopt every orphan, feed every family, or support missionaries in every country. So how can you decide what God is calling you to do?

Start with your call. Your first obligation is to care for those God has entrusted to your care. True religion starts at home, with your nuclear and church family. Paul told Timothy not to give special assistance to widows who have "children or grandchildren," for "these should learn first of all to put their religion into practice by caring for their own family and so repaying their parents and grandparents." Paul concluded, "Anyone who does not provide for their relatives, and especially for their own household, has denied the faith and is worse than an unbeliever" (1 Tim. 5:4 – 8).

We must make sure our own house is in order if we are to extend ourselves into the world. We need healthy families to adopt children into, financially secure individuals who can share their wealth with others, and caring churches that tend to their own members so that together they can reach out to the community. Paul explained this near-and-far responsibility when he commanded, "Therefore, as we have opportunity, let us do good to all people, especially to those who belong to the family of believers" (Gal. 6:10). We have a covenantal obligation to serve those who belong to our church family, but always with an eye on the wider world. We "warn those who are idle and disruptive, encourage the disheartened, help the weak," so that as one body we might do such good deeds that even the "pagans" will "glorify God on the day he visits us" (1 Thess. 5:14; 1 Peter 2:12).

> WE HAVE A COVENANTAL OBLIGATION TO SERVE THOSE WHO BELONG TO OUR CHURCH FAMILY, BUT ALWAYS WITH AN EYE ON THE WIDER WORLD.

It helps me to prioritize my family and church when I remember that, for all our ambitious talk about "changing the world," we only ever deeply matter to a handful of people. You can be a president or a pauper, a celebrity or a commoner, and roughly the same number of people will cry at your funeral. Make sure they are the right ones.

Once you are confident that you are fulfilling your covenantal obligations, you then are free to consider other opportunities. You must, or you will squander the many resources God has entrusted to you. Like Abraham of old, God has blessed you so you can bless others (Gen. 12:1 – 3). As any giver can tell you, blessing others is the best way to be blessed yourself. Our church and family suffocate when we lean inward and inhale the same stale air. When we turn around and face the world, the fresh breeze from outside blows in and invigorates our relationships. Our covenantal obligations may be most important, but they need room to breathe. They need the higher purpose that comes only from serving Jesus in the world.

This does not mean we will fix every problem or meet every need. Jesus didn't heal every leper and personally talk to every unbeliever, and he conceded, "The poor you will always have with you" (Mark 14:7). But we will be able to help many, perhaps more than we thought possible, if we begin with our callings and build up and out with those in our covenant communities. The fall and its damage won't be erased until Jesus returns, but we can make a start. When people look at our lives, our families, and our churches, may they point their finger and say, "Something like that. When Jesus returns, the entire world is going to look something like that."

# PART 4

# REDEMPTION

The gospel is the best news you'll ever hear, yet it intensifies the tension you feel between your human and Christian life. The good news of salvation is like desperately needed medical supplies dropped into a war zone. These supplies are the answer to many prayers, yet if you are a triage surgeon, your work is just beginning. Whom do you treat first? How do you prevent burnout, especially if the need is overwhelming? How can you possibly take a break from surgery knowing that so many lives hang in the balance? But how can you not take periods of rest, especially considering you will not be able to help them all?

Jesus said, "The harvest is plentiful, but the workers are few. Ask the Lord of the harvest, therefore, to send out workers into his harvest field" (Luke 10:2). If you obey Jesus' command to make disciples, then you are an answer to this prayer. Good for Jesus and great for the people who desperately still need to be saved. But what about the burden you feel? How can you reconcile the urgency of the gospel with the demands of being human? Can you serve Jesus and still enjoy your life?

# CHAPTER 17

# GOSPEL

The gospel is the good news about what *God* has done.
*D. A. Carson*

What is the gospel? This is a crucial question for evangelical Christians, so we tend to argue about it every thirty years. In the late eighties, we debated lordship salvation: Must Jesus be your Lord to also be your Savior, or was lordship an optional step of obedience for those who already were saved? One side argued against cheap grace while the other warned against corrupting the gospel with works. I was in seminary at the time, and my missions professor shared that in a recent international summit one of the foreign pastors stood and said with a sigh, "When you Americans figure out what the gospel is, will you please come tell us?"

Ouch! This lordship salvation debate has returned with the rise of radical Christianity. David Platt's *Radical* rightly corrects the cheap grace often found in American evangelicalism, where churchgoers who live like their non-Christian neighbors nevertheless assume they're saved just because they've said the sinner's prayer. Yet Platt's emphasis on Jesus' call to discipleship leaves some readers worried they haven't sacrificed enough to be saved. He explains:

After writing *Radical,* I received all kinds of questions and comments about specific facets of the Christian life in America. People would ask me, "What does a radical lifestyle look like? What kind of car should I drive, or should I even drive a car? What kind of house should I live in? Am I supposed to adopt? Am I supposed to move overseas to a foreign mission field?"

I found these questions, though sincere and honest, to be a bit troubling. It felt like people were looking for a box to check or a criterion to follow that would ensure they were obeying God. But such questions, if we're not careful, bypass the core of what it means to follow Jesus. Outside of the commands of Christ in Scripture, we have no specific set of rules or regulations regarding how the radical commands of Christ apply to our lives. Instead, we have a relationship with Jesus.[1]

This entire book that you have in your hands attempts to help solve this problem, explaining how we may follow Jesus as Lord without falling into the trap of legalism. We can and we must integrate the redemptive command to make disciples with the normal pleasures of creation. As we've seen time and again, it comes down to vocation. We're all called to follow Jesus, yet we follow him in different tasks and responsibilities, according to our gifts, desires, and opportunities.

> WE CAN AND WE MUST INTEGRATE THE REDEMPTIVE COMMAND TO MAKE DISCIPLES WITH THE NORMAL PLEASURES OF CREATION.

Besides this perennial question on lordship salvation, another recurring debate asks whether the gospel focuses on individual persons or the entire world. Theologically conservative churches consistently emphasize the personal aspect of the gospel, saying the good news is that Jesus died to forgive our sins and reconcile us to God. In the flagship book of the Gospel

Coalition (a network of conservative evangelical pastors), Bryan Chapell writes, "A good summary of the gospel is 'Christ Jesus came into the world to save sinners' (1 Tim. 1:15)."[2]

Other scholars, such as N. T. Wright and Scot McKnight, argue that this plan of personal salvation is not the gospel. The gospel is the larger cosmic truth that Jesus is Lord. He is Israel's Messiah who perfectly kept Israel's covenant, enabling God's people to become the kingdom of priests that humans always were intended to be. The gospel includes the offer of personal salvation — so this is not unimportant — but it is specifically about the much larger story of creation, fall, and redemption. The gospel is not narrowly about how individual sinners can avoid hell and be reconciled to God, but about how the Lord Jesus is redeeming the whole world.[3]

## DEEP AND WIDE

Supporters of this big-picture gospel note that when the apostles define the gospel, they do not give the Romans Road steps to salvation but rather speak of the events of Christ's life and how they fulfill Israel's longing for the kingdom. In 1 Corinthians 15:1 – 5, Paul said the gospel is that Christ died, was buried, was raised, and appeared to his followers, "according to the Scriptures" that Israel followed. In Romans 1:1 – 5, Paul said the gospel is about the Lord Jesus, "a descendant of David," who by his resurrection was declared to be "the Son of God" who unites Gentiles and Jews into the family of God. And in Acts 10:36 – 38, Peter told Cornelius that "the good news of peace" began when Jesus proved he was "Lord of all" by "doing good and healing all who were under the power of the devil."

The big-picture gospelers say the gospel of personal salvation is too small. It is so focused on how individual sinners can get into heaven that it misses the larger story of Israel, the church, and how the entire universe finally will be redeemed. The gospel is more expansive and exhilarating than most Christians realize.

It is not merely about the salvation of your soul but the resurrection of your body too. Jesus came to rescue all of you. And not just you, but also your family, society, and the earth itself.

> JESUS CAME TO RESCUE ALL OF YOU. AND NOT JUST YOU, BUT ALSO YOUR FAMILY, SOCIETY, AND THE EARTH ITSELF.

This big picture reminds us that we must never be content to make converts who believe they are going to heaven merely because they said the sinner's prayer. Rather, we must make disciples who obediently live in the kingdom that Jesus has established. The gospel is larger than believing that the cross of Christ forgives our sin. It includes embracing the entire story of Jesus — his life, death, and resurrection — which inspires us to kingdom living until he returns.

The big-picture gospel sounds a lot like what I am arguing for in this book. I heartily embrace its emphasis on the cosmic redemption and reign of Jesus Christ. But we must be careful lest its panoramic vision of the whole obscures Scripture's equal focus on our personal need for salvation. The gospel is about more than individual salvation, but it is not less. Look again at the passages that advocate a big-picture gospel. In 1 Corinthians 15:1 – 5, Paul did not merely say that Jesus died "according to the Scriptures," but also that he died "for our sins" (v. 3). In Romans 1:16, Paul concluded his introduction to the gospel by declaring, "It is the power of God that brings salvation to everyone who believes." And in Acts 10:43, Peter told Cornelius that the upshot of the gospel of Jesus is that "everyone who believes in him receives forgiveness of sins through his name." The gospel declares Jesus is Lord and, for that reason, urges all people to repent of their sin and submit to him.

This emphasis on personal salvation is essential for preserving the gospel. When we say the gospel is only that Jesus is Lord, we are tempted to think we contribute to the gospel whenever we serve Christ's kingdom in the world. So we repeat the mantra, "Share the gospel at all times, and if necessary, use words." This saying reminds us that our actions matter, but it confuses kingdom living with the gospel. The gospel is good *news*, and news must be spoken. It can also be written, but when we have really good news, we still prefer to call rather than text. Either way, we can't mime the gospel. We have to use our words.

Worse, when we conflate kingdom living with the gospel, the latter is no longer about the redemptive events of Jesus' life — good news we *receive* — but about the many good things we can *achieve*. So we talk about the gospel of social justice, racial reconciliation, or creation care. These are all important facets of kingdom living, but they are not called the gospel anywhere in Scripture. The gospel is the message about what God has done in Jesus and what he will yet do. Period. Full stop. We don't contribute anything at all.

Understanding our utter dependence on God also helps to reconcile our responsibility to share the gospel with our need to lead a normal life. We are surrounded by people who are likely headed to hell. How can we pass by any without telling them about Jesus? When I was in college, I heard a few sermons from Ezekiel 33:8 that implied God would hold me accountable if I didn't explain the plan of salvation to an unbeliever who then died without hearing about Jesus. I often drove my gospel team's van, and I remember feeling enormous pressure (not directly from them) to put a tract on top of the cash I handed to the tollbooth operator.

> THE GOSPEL IS THE MESSAGE ABOUT WHAT GOD HAS DONE IN JESUS AND WHAT HE WILL YET DO. PERIOD.

Now I'm a lot less stressed. I still pray for opportunities to tell others about Jesus, for nothing is more important than rescuing a person from everlasting damnation. My happiest moments are when I'm explaining the gospel to people who have not yet put their faith in Christ. Yet I also know God doesn't hold me responsible for bringing the world to him. Even Jesus didn't heal every leper or lead everyone to salvation, yet he still claimed he had finished the work his Father had sent him to do (John 17:4). God's sovereign grace compels me to evangelize, because I know God may use my words to bring sinners to himself. God's sovereign grace also frees me to play, exercise, and sleep, because I know the success of the gospel does not ultimately depend on me.

## WHAT IS THE GOSPEL?

Since the gospel means good news, an easy way to understand it is to start with the bad news. What is the problem the gospel aims to fix? In the opening chapter of the Gospel According to Matthew, the angel told Joseph to name his Son Jesus "because he will save his people from their sins" (1:21). Paul agreed, writing, "Christ Jesus came into the world to save sinners — of whom I am the worst" (1 Tim. 1:15). Peter told the Sanhedrin that God had exalted Jesus "to his own right hand as Prince and Savior that he might bring Israel to repentance and forgive their sins" (Acts 5:31).

The bad news starts with our sin. Watch out for euphemisms that tone down this fact. One popular song says we need forgiveness "'cause we all make mistakes sometimes, and we all step across that line."[4] Another says Jesus has come to "fix my broken life."[5] We *are* broken people who make mistakes, but this is not why we need forgiveness. A mistake is forgetting to carry the 1 on a math test. Broken is what happens to your window when you play baseball inside. Jesus did not die on the cross, as one preacher said, to save us from "brokenness, loneliness, and low self-esteem." These are symptoms of a much deeper problem, which the Bible calls sin. We must treat this root cause, or its troubling effects will never go away.

Every generation must find fresh words to describe sin's sting. The word *sin* itself no longer communicates the point, as our culture uses it as a snicker word to describe desserts, soap operas, and other guilty pleasures. A previous generation said we are "rebels" who are "morally bankrupt," but these terms do not carry the stigma they once did. Today there is no shame in erasing your debts and starting over, and who doesn't want to be a little wild and out of control? I still prefer the biblical term *sin*, especially when it is pushed aside by tepid imposters like *broken* and *mistakes*, but I explain that it means that left to ourselves we are selfish, despicable traitors who would murder God if we had the chance. This is not mere speculation, for the one time God gave us an opening, we took it.

The bad news may start with us humans, but it doesn't end there. Our loathsome mutiny against God went viral and ravaged the rest of creation, which now groans "in eager expectation for the children of God to be revealed." The world longs for the return of Christ when "the creation itself will be liberated from its bondage to decay and brought into the freedom and glory of the children of God" (Rom. 8:19 – 22). If the good news corresponds to this bad news, then we must follow Martyn Lloyd-Jones's advice to "present the total Gospel. There is a personal side to it; we must deal with that, and we must start with that. But we do not stop with that; there is a social side, indeed a cosmic side as well. We must present the whole plan of salvation as it is revealed in the Scriptures."[6]

What is the gospel? It is good news for the *world*. New Testament scholar Michael Bird explains: The gospel is "the announcement that God's kingdom has come in the life, death, and resurrection of Jesus of Nazareth, the Lord and Messiah, in fulfillment of Israel's Scriptures."[7] And it is good news for *sinners*. The gospel is the promise that all who repent and trust entirely in Jesus for the forgiveness of sin will receive the gift of the Holy Spirit, be united to Jesus and to his church, and reign with Jesus when he returns to reconcile all things and consummate his glorious kingdom. We will examine what this means for us next.

# CHAPTER 18

# KINGDOM

All dualism is eschewed in the unity of God's theocratic rule.
*Herman Bavinck*

I t's Saturday. I plan to write a few pages in the morning, grade papers in the afternoon, and watch a football game tonight. My wife is running loads of laundry and helping my daughter rearrange her room for the second time this month. At some point, we'll probably sneak in a family game of Mario Kart or Sorry. If all goes according to plan, we won't even leave the house.

My life seems rather ordinary, even stationary, so I'm troubled when I read Jesus' commands for his followers to get up and move. "Come." "Leave." "Follow me." Jesus walked down to the Sea of Galilee and called to Peter and Andrew, " 'Come, follow me ... and I will send you out to fish for people.' At once they left their nets and followed him." Jesus continued along the shore and saw James and John, who were helping their father prepare their nets. He "called them, and immediately they left the boat and their father and followed him" (Matt. 4:19 – 22).

Jesus demanded that his disciples follow him right away, and he showed a surprising lack of grace to those who had good reasons to ask for time or understanding. When one potential disciple asked if first he could bury his father, Jesus replied, "Follow me, and let the dead bury their own dead" (Matt. 8:22). When a wealthy young man asked how he could have everlasting life, he was told, "Sell everything you have and give to the poor.... Then come, follow me" (Luke 18:22). The man went away shaking his head, for in that Middle Eastern society his possessions also belonged to his extended family. How could he sell their ancestral home for a stranger he had just met?[1]

These calls for radical commitment leave me wondering if my ordinary life is sufficiently Christian. Are grading papers, keeping house, and playing with my children all God wants from me today? Is my normal human life enough?

## DUAL CITIZENS

It helps to remember the disciples were in a unique situation. When the Son of God stands before you and invites you to join the mission that will save the world, you drop your nets and go! This once-in-a-forever opportunity was infinitely more urgent than catching fish. And yet a week or so after the resurrection, when seven of the disciples were hanging out, Peter said, "'I'm going out to fish'... and they said, 'We'll go with you'" (John 21:3).

How could Peter and the disciples fish at a time like this? Well, it gave them something to do. Even more, it was what they did. They were fishermen. They could sit around in a windowless room and wait for the risen Christ to appear, or they could wait while they fished. They were fishermen, so they went to sea.

Our situation is similar. Jesus is not standing before us, urging us to leave our family and follow him around the countryside. Like Peter, we are waiting for the risen Christ to reappear. And like Peter, we serve Jesus not by leaving our nets but by returning to them. Jesus may call you to change careers and become a missionary, as he did eventually with Peter, but in the meantime you answer his call by diligently doing whatever it is you do. Are you a fishermen, florist, or forklift operator? This is your field to serve Jesus.

Of course, these creational callings are relativized by the risen Christ. Peter knew Someone who was far more important than fishing, so I doubt it bothered him much when he fished all night and caught nothing. It might be nice to catch something and make a little money, but it certainly wasn't necessary. Jesus was alive! Sin and death had been defeated forever, and just last week! Everything else was gravy. This is why, when Peter realized whom the man was who told them to cast their nets on the other side, he left their bulging nets behind, leaped into the water and splashed to his Lord.

> JESUS MAY CALL YOU TO CHANGE CAREERS AND BECOME A MISSIONARY ... BUT IN THE MEANTIME YOU ANSWER HIS CALL BY DILIGENTLY DOING WHATEVER IT IS YOU DO.

The risen Christ not only relativizes our callings, but he also reclaims them. Once the boat had beached, Jesus told Peter to bring some of the fish they had caught, so Peter "climbed back into the boat and dragged the net ashore. It was full of large fish, 153, but even with so many the net was not torn" (John 21:11). Jesus doesn't take away our callings; he empowers us to thrive in them. Notice that these devoted disciples never stopped being fishermen. They were thrilled to be in the presence of Jesus, the Friend and Savior they had seen only twice since his resurrection, yet someone kept the presence of mind to count the fish — all 153! Does it matter how many fish you've caught when you're rejoicing in the glory of Jesus? It does if you're a fisherman.

Jesus used their fish to serve breakfast, an act of hospitality that set the table for his reconciliation with Peter. While the callings of creation and redemption are distinct, they mutually serve each other in the unified reign of Jesus. And yet they *are* distinct. The kingdom of God is Jesus' rightful rule over his world as its Creator and Redeemer. As Creator, Jesus commands all people to govern this world on his behalf, managing the animals and developing nature's raw materials into a flourishing culture

(Gen. 1:28; 2:15). As Redeemer, Jesus commands his followers to go into the world and make disciples of all nations (Matt. 28:19).

Christians inhabit the kingdom as dual citizens. As humans we are citizens of this world, so we join our non-Christian neighbors to improve education, the economy, and the environment. We vote and volunteer in our community because we realize, as the anthem from *High School Musical* says, "We're All in This Together."[2] Like the Jewish exiles in Babylon, we obey God's command to "seek the peace and prosperity of the city" and "pray to the LORD for it, because if it prospers, you too will prosper" (Jer. 29:7).

As Christians we remember the kingdom of God is not of this world. We celebrate the kingdom's central focus on redemption when we gather as the body of Christ to hear God's Word, receive the sacraments, and respond with worship, prayers, and communion with God's people. The church is the headquarters of God's kingdom on earth. It is the main way his rule is honored and advanced in the world. And since God's reign includes both creation and redemption, it is not surprising to find the church addressing both of these, but in different ways.

## DUAL CHURCH

Dutch statesman and theologian Abraham Kuyper helpfully divided the responsibilities for redemption and creation between what he called the church as institution and the church as organism.[3] The institutional church is the formal organization that gathers to worship God and celebrate his personal and corporate salvation. This gathered church must emphasize redemption, how Jesus saves us from hell and unites us with other believers in his body. We come together to preach the gospel, baptize, share the Lord's Supper, and lovingly discipline those who have fallen into sin. If we ever lose our heart for redemption, we will become just another social club or philanthropic organization. We may do some good in the world, but we will no longer be authentically Christian.

The church as organism is Kuyper's term for individual Christians who either separately or in groups promote the lordship of Christ in their various callings.[4] These Christian laborers are an extension of the church. They are not detached individuals who act on their own but on behalf of the King who sent them into society to serve their neighbors and responsibly develop culture.[5] If these scattered Christians ever lose this emphasis on creation — if they attempt to use their jobs as nothing more than a launchpad for evangelism — they will annoy others and bring ridicule on the name of Christ. They also will likely be fired, for they will be talking about Jesus when they should have been working.

The tasks of the gathered institutional church and scattered individual Christians are distinct, but they are not mutually exclusive. Individual Christians who diligently do their jobs and seek their neighbor's good build a platform from which they can winsomely talk about Jesus. When people ask what motivates them, they can explain the gospel and invite them to church. Peter had this in mind when he told Christian women to submit to their unbelieving husbands so they "may be won over without words by the behavior of their wives, when they see the purity and reverence of your lives" (1 Peter 3:1 – 2). And Paul urged preachers to "Teach slaves to be subject to their masters in everything, to try to please them, not to talk back to them, and not to steal from them, but to show that they can be fully trusted, so that in every way they will make the teaching about God our Savior attractive" (Titus 2:9 – 10).

CHRISTIANS WHO DILIGENTLY DO THEIR JOBS AND SEEK THEIR NEIGHBOR'S GOOD BUILD A PLATFORM FROM WHICH THEY CAN WINSOMELY TALK ABOUT JESUS.

Paul's command also illustrates how the institutional church serves individual Christians. The church gathers to celebrate redemption, but it also educates and exhorts believers to view their work in creation as divine callings. If Christians are the salt of the earth, then the church is a resalinization plant that rejuvenates the salt before sprinkling it back across society. Biblical preaching explains how the gospel transforms daily life — marriage, money, friendships, and vocation — which in turn brings attention to the gospel. As Peter encouraged Christians, "Live such good lives among the pagans that, though they accuse you of doing wrong, they may see your good deeds and glorify God on the day he visits us" (1 Peter 2:12). When flourishing Christians credit Jesus, they lead people back to the institutional church, and the virtuous cycle is complete.

**Figure 18.1: How the Church Serves the Kingdom**

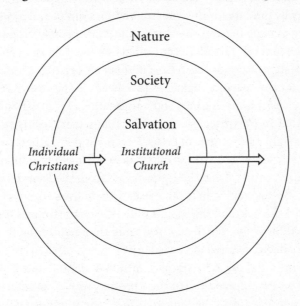

Besides inspiring individual believers to serve Christ in the world, the institutional church itself should look for ways to help those who are suffering from poverty or injustice. This can be dangerous, as our compassion for people's physical problems may easily swamp our concern for their spiritual needs. Many churches that began social programs as an outreach of the gospel became so excited about feeding and clothing the poor that they forgot to share Jesus with them. They began to assume the gospel and, in a generation or two, had lost it entirely. We must also recognize our limitations. Even Jesus didn't meet every physical need but conceded "the poor you will always have with you" (Matt. 26:11).

But we must do *something*. James said real faith feeds and clothes our brothers and sisters and looks "after orphans and widows in their distress" (James 1:27; 2:14 – 17).

The early church accepted James's challenge and did so much good that by the end of the second century, Tertullian could argue that Christians were Rome's best citizens. They supported society by praying for the emperor and his empire and by giving money to orphans and shut-ins and to bury people too poor to afford a funeral. Tertullian concluded that the Roman world suffered a significant loss each time it killed a Christian.[6]

Our helping hand might also turn heads to the gospel. In *The Rise of Christianity*, Rodney Stark argues that the Christian faith exploded in part because early Christians sacrificially helped their neighbors in times of crisis. Pagan religion had no answer for the deadly plague that struck North Africa in the middle of the third century. Even their priests fled from the contaminated cities. But average Christians risked their lives to nurse and comfort the sick, and the pagans noticed. Stark estimates that by the middle of the fourth century, more than half of the Roman Empire had converted to Christianity.[7]

Many of these Christians continued their helping ways. When a new emperor, Julian the Apostate, wanted to return the empire to paganism, he lamented that "the impious Galileans support not only their own poor but ours as well, all men see that our people lack aid from us."[8] It's difficult to persuade people to become pagans when continually their next meal comes from Christians.

Our concern for others must be genuine. I once heard a pastor explain why his church was starting a program to feed the poor. He must have been worried that some might think he was promoting a "social gospel," because he said the only reason they were doing this ministry was to reach more people for Christ. I winced when I heard this. I wondered what the people who were being helped would have thought if they had been there. Wouldn't they have felt the church didn't really care about them, but was merely using their hunger as bait to get their souls?

IT'S DIFFICULT TO PERSUADE PEOPLE TO BECOME PAGANS WHEN CONTINUALLY THEIR NEXT MEAL COMES FROM CHRISTIANS.

There are dangers on both sides as we seek to faithfully bear witness to the kingdom. Jesus is Lord of creation and redemption, and he deserves our best in each sphere. We joyfully inhabit the kingdom when we share our faith or join our hearts for corporate worship, and we still inhabit the kingdom, perhaps a little less joyfully, when we stay home to do laundry and grade papers. This kingdom is both here and on its way, which produces another tension we will examine next.

# CHAPTER 19

# ALREADY BUT NOT YET

It is already the time of the end, and yet is not *the* end.... The present period of the Church is the time between the decisive battle, which has already occurred, and the "Victory Day."

*Oscar Cullman*

John the Baptist had reason to be radical. He knew that his birth had been a miracle and that an angel had told his aged father that John would be a new Elijah who would prepare the way for the Messiah. He knew by heart the prophecy his father had sung at his birth, especially the lines that promised God would rescue his people from the hand of their enemies (Luke 1:5 – 17, 67 – 79). And soon enough he would see the Spirit of God descending on Jesus and hear God say, "This is my Son, whom I love; with him I am well pleased" (Matt. 3:17).

So it's no surprise John was all in. He dressed and ate the part of Elijah — living in the wilderness on locusts and wild honey — and he displayed a similar contempt for Israel's leaders. When curious Pharisees and Sadducees came out to see him, John greeted them with "You brood of vipers! Who warned you to flee from the coming wrath?" He told them this was their last chance to repent. They would either be baptized with water today or fire tomorrow, and he wouldn't lose sleep either way. John knew he was on the right side of history. If they wished to join him, they had better produce fruit that proved their repentance, because "the ax is already at the root of the trees, and every tree that does not produce good fruit will be cut down and thrown into the fire" (Matt. 3:7 – 12).

Like Elijah before him, John's take-no-prisoners approach landed him in trouble with the king's wife (she didn't appreciate being called an adulteress), and she had him thrown into jail. John's confidence took a hit. His disciples fed him stories about what Jesus was up to, which made him more depressed. Jesus had told his hometown that he was the embodiment of Isaiah's prophecy:

> The Spirit of the Sovereign LORD is on me,
>> because the LORD has anointed me
>> to proclaim good news to the poor.
> He has sent me to bind up the brokenhearted,
>> to proclaim freedom for the captives
>> and release from darkness for the prisoners,
> to proclaim the year of the LORD's favor. (Isa. 61:1 – 2)

Uh-oh. Why did Jesus stop reading there? What about the very next line, which says the Messiah will proclaim "the day of vengeance of our God"? Where is the "winnowing fork" that "will burn up the chaff with unquenchable fire"? Where is the promised judgment that will vanquish God's enemies? (Luke 3:17; 4:18 – 19).

John must have been thinking, *Jesus, don't go soft on me. I did my job. I stuck my neck out for you, warning everyone you were coming to knock heads and establish your kingdom. Let's finish this thing. You do know who you are, right?* Just to be sure, John sent two of his disciples to ask the Lord, "Are you the one who is to come, or should we expect someone else?" (Luke 7:19).

Jesus sent them back with a summary of Isaiah's prophecy, again with the warnings of judgment removed. Of course I'm the

Messiah, Jesus implied. "The blind receive sight, the lame walk, those who have leprosy are cleansed, the deaf hear, the dead are raised, and the good news is proclaimed to the poor." Oh, and John, "Blessed is anyone who does not stumble on account of me" (Luke 7:18 – 23).

**LIKE AN ENGAGED COUPLE WAITING FOR THE CONSUMMATION OF THEIR MARRIAGE, WE LIVE IN THE AWKWARD MOMENT "BETWEEN THE TIMES."**

John wasn't wrong. He was just early. In chapter 4, I explained that the one story of God contains two important distinctions: between the natural and the supernatural and between creation and redemption. Here is a third distinction, occurring within redemption itself.

Redemption has already begun, but it's not yet finished. Jesus said, "The kingdom of God has come upon you" (Matt. 12:28), so in some sense his kingdom is already here (Mark 1:15). Yet he also taught us to pray, "Your kingdom come" (Matt. 6:10), so in another sense it is still on its way. Like an engaged couple waiting for the consummation of their marriage, we live in the awkward moment "between the times." The kingdom has been established, but it has not yet been completed (Rev. 11:15). We must honor both parts.

## KUYPER'S KINGDOM

Besides the controversies surrounding the gospel (see chapter 17), evangelical pastors and theologians are also debating the nature of the kingdom. The discussion centers on this question: Is there one kingdom of God that governs both the church and the world, or does God have two kingdoms, one for the world and another for the church?

Those who believe in a single kingdom say this explains why Jesus is Lord of all. If the kingdom embraces everything, then nothing lies beyond the scope of redemption. Al Wolters expounds this exhilarating vision:

> If Christ is the reconciler of all things, and if we have been entrusted with "the ministry of reconciliation" on his behalf (2 Cor. 5:18), then we have a redemptive task wherever our vocation places us in his world. No invisible dividing line within creation limits the applicability of such basic biblical concepts as reconciliation, redemption, salvation, sanctification, renewal, the kingdom of God, and so on. In the name of Christ, distortion must be opposed *everywhere* — in the kitchen and the bedroom, in city councils and corporate boardrooms, on the stage and on the air, in the classroom and in the workshop. Everywhere creation calls for the honoring of God's standards.[1]

Neal Plantinga adds that the kingdom begins in the church and then spills over into the world. We serve the kingdom when we gather for worship, and we also serve the kingdom in our callings, particularly when we play

> a lively part in institutions and endeavors that, consciously or not, *seek the interests of the kingdom*. Of these the church is first, but others — including governments, businesses, professions, and nonprofit service organizations — are crucial as well. So are families. If they work right, *families become a microcosm of the kingdom of God*, incubating us in faith, hope, and love, schooling us in patience, supplying us with memories good enough to take out of storage on a lonely night.[2]

No act is too trivial to be excluded from the kingdom. Plantinga says we serve the kingdom not only by praying and taking Communion but also by flying kites and baking bread, reading good books and playing good music, and resting. Some Christians

> join volunteer groups that turn rails to trails, or that assist flood victims, or that paint somebody's house. In an emergency, an adult Christian might spend herself for a friend

who is dying — sitting with her, praying with her, encouraging her, seeing to some of her needs. This isn't a job that appears on any government list of occupations, but it is a calling of God, and *it is surely a contribution to the kingdom of God.*[3]

Wolters and Plantinga learned this unified vision from earlier Dutch Reformed thinkers such as Abraham Kuyper, so this view is often called the Kuyperian world and life view.[4] It has two main strengths: It easily integrates our human and Christian lives under the reign of Christ, and it emphasizes this kingdom is already here. We need not worry that any task is too insignificant to contribute to the kingdom. Wherever you are and whatever you're doing, do it for the King and it counts.

The weaknesses of this Kuyperian vision correspond to its strengths. It is possible to overplay the integration between redemption and creation, the church and the world, so we no longer privilege what is most important. Some denominations have overlearned the Kuyperian emphasis on the unity of the kingdom, and their members often skip church for a day at the beach, give more money to disaster relief than traditional missions, and choose every other calling except gospel ministry.[5] Others have allowed worldly concerns to subvert the primary mission of the institutional church. Their annual conventions pass resolutions that oppose bullying and mountaintop removal coal mining and support tax reform and carbon-neutral church buildings.[6] Is this all the kingdom of God amounts to?

> WE NEED NOT WORRY THAT ANY TASK IS TOO INSIGNIFICANT TO CONTRIBUTE TO THE KINGDOM.... WHATEVER YOU'RE DOING, DO IT FOR THE KING AND IT COUNTS.

Stressing that the kingdom is already here also poses a danger. Some Christians think Jesus faces long odds in the world today. The world is overrun with so much immorality and injustice that they assume the church is losing. Then they meet cheery Christians who tell them to chin up because the kingdom is all around them. They share stories of community gardens, picnics in the park, and the latest attempt to upgrade schools (free iPads for fifth graders!). But this encouragement turns out to be just a longer route to pessimism. A discerning person might wonder, *So the kingdom is already here, huh? Then this is as good as it gets?* We live well "between the times" when we remember two things: The kingdom is already here, so be positive. But the kingdom isn't all the way here, so don't gush.

> THE KINGDOM IS ALREADY HERE, SO BE POSITIVE. BUT THE KINGDOM ISN'T ALL THE WAY HERE, SO DON'T GUSH.

## TWO KINGDOMS

An alternate approach claims that God rules the church and the world in two separate kingdoms. The two kingdoms view avoids the Kuyperian temptation toward false equivalence (everything is more or less equal) and triumphalism (we can transform the culture!) by saying the church is more important than the world and the future kingdom far surpasses what is here now. Michael Horton explains Jesus is Lord over both the world and the church — *but in different ways.* Jesus the Creator rules the world through his civil kingdom of common grace. He commands Christians to join their fellow humans in contributing to culture, but he doesn't ask them to "transform their workplace, neighborhood, or nation into the kingdom of Christ." The kingdom of Christ is found only in the church, where Jesus the Redeemer rules by "Word, sacrament, and covenantal nurture." We cannot build this kingdom through our cultural efforts, but can only receive it through "baptism, preaching, teaching, Eucharist, prayer, and fellowship" as we await its consummation when Jesus returns.[7]

Here's what the two kingdoms view says about us: As humans we participate in creation like everyone else. We aren't called to redeem our jobs or discover the Christian way to do math or fix a carburetor. We don't need to justify oil painting, cabinetmaking, or landscaping by how they contribute to the kingdom of Christ. They don't, and that's okay. We do these cultural tasks because we are human, not because they somehow restore creation or transform the culture for Christ. As Christians we also belong to the church, a sacred community that proclaims the only gospel that will save the world. So while we do our fair share of common cultural work, we reserve our highest allegiance for the church and the kingdom that Jesus is building there.[8]

Two strengths of the two kingdoms view are its priority on redemption and the return of Christ. It is right to remind us that the church is the center of the kingdom, and that this kingdom will not shine in all its brilliance until the consummation of all things. Only Jesus can bring in the kingdom. We must wait for it.

And yet these two strengths also generate corresponding weaknesses. If Kuyperians risk running too much together, proponents of the two kingdoms risk keeping too much apart. We must distinguish creation and redemption, world and church, and our human and Christian lives, but we cannot separate them without producing a sacred-secular split. If the kingdom of Christ is only found in the church, it's easy to devalue the importance of cultural work in the world. Why study law, geometry, and auto mechanics when you could be serving the kingdom instead? Whatever you do in the world will be erased anyway when Jesus returns to consummate his kingdom. David Van Drunen explains, "The affairs of human culture are temporary, provisional, and bound to pass away.... Cultural activity remains important for Christians, but it will come to an abrupt end, along with this present world as a whole, when Christ returns and cataclysmically ushers in the new heaven and new earth."[9]

The two kingdoms' insistence on separating the church from the world also hamstrings the church's witness. A church that must stay in its own lane and not interfere with the world cannot easily fight for social justice. Muffled in part by a Lutheran version of the two kingdoms, the German church said little as the Nazis rose to power. Likewise, churches cannot organize against racism, slavery, or abortion without violating the foundational principle of the two kingdoms. This is a problem.

## CAREFUL KUYPERIANISM

Dialogue between the two camps has encouraged both sides to find common ground. They may speak with a different accent, but most participants on either side agree we both must prioritize the church (because of redemption) and do good in the world (because of creation).[10] Here is my attempt to incorporate the best of both worlds, combining two kingdoms insights into a Kuyperian view.

**Figure 19.1: How the Kingdom Exists in the World**

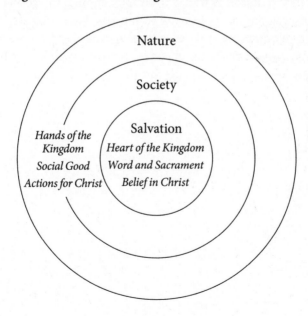

The institutional church is the heart of God's Kingdom on earth (with a capital K), for it is where rebellious sinners hear the Word and submit to the lordship of Christ. Jesus is destroying Satan's kingdom, not primarily through Christian books or bumper stickers (especially not them), but by his church, which he promised would storm the gates of hell (Matt. 16:18). But though God's Kingdom is headquartered in his church, it is larger than the gathering of God's people. When citizens of the kingdom scatter into their communities, they take the kingdom with them. They submit to Jesus in every area of life, not only in their weekly worship but also in their homes, jobs, and neighborhoods. Just as Jesus established his kingdom by exorcising demons and healing the sick, so they reveal the rule of God when they root out the many ways sin has contaminated their world (Matt. 4:23 – 25; 10:1 – 8; 12:28).

The kingdom is already here, so we boldly step out and speak up for Jesus. The kingdom also is not yet, so we must await its full arrival. We choose to wait actively, proclaiming the gospel and performing the sort of just and loving acts that anticipate Jesus' return. We don't presume we will change the world, but we hope to make a world of change in our corner of creation. May what is already here whet our appetite for what is yet to come.

# CHAPTER 20

# NEW EARTH

God does not make junk, and he does not junk what he
has made.

*Albert Wolters*

I was privileged to grow up in churches that taught the Word
of God. I learned my Bible well. I also learned one big mistake
in reading it. We often confused things with actions (see chapter
7) and put down creation to promote redemption. We regularly
said, "There are only two things in this world that last forever:
the Word of God and souls. Everything else is going to burn, so
live for what matters most."

I left worship services determined to spend less time on temporal distractions and more time on eternal matters. Yet I still had
to take exams, go to work, and practice my trumpet. I gave most
of my week to activities that didn't seem to make an eternal difference and then gathered with friends on Sunday to feel bad about it.
I told myself I would do better next time, but by Monday morning
I was already focused on the homework that would fill my week.

I didn't know how to break out of this cycle of spiritual guilt,
so I subconsciously separated my Christian and human life. I
knew I should be more focused on eternity, and I rightly made
time for daily devotions. But often this was as far as I got. My

Christian disciplines became little more than an add-on, something I tacked onto the front or back end of each day. Bible study and prayer lifted me above and beyond my normal life, but they didn't seem to make much difference in it. I felt close to God as I meditated on his Word, but when I closed the Bible I fell back immediately into the whirl of the temporal world.

Then I went to college, where my history professor, James McGoldrick, taught me the Reformers had figured out how to integrate the Christian faith into their normal human lives. I learned more about this in seminary when Professor Jim Grier used Al Wolters's book *Creation Regained* to explain the biblical story of creation, fall, and redemption. *This changes everything!* I thought. It's still true that the Word of God and souls will last forever, but so will bodies and much of the planet. If redemption restores creation, then creation counts for more than I had ever suspected.

I wrote about this in my first book, *Heaven Is a Place on Earth*, and am glad to recommend other books on the subject, such as Neal Plantinga's *Engaging God's World*, N. T. Wright's *Surprised by Hope*, and Randy Alcorn's *Heaven*. These books emphasize the continuity between this world and the next and explain that our final destination is a new earth rather than a celestial heaven (the title of Alcorn's book is misleading). Lately some two kingdoms theologians have begun to push back, saying this world is not our final home but will burn up in a cosmic conflagration. The only things that will survive from this world to the next are the Word of God and people.[1] So we are nearly right back where we started.

This chapter will get us on track by answering two questions: "What will the new earth be like?" and "How is it connected to this one?" We have more questions than answers, but we know enough to long for Christ's return and the restoration of this creation.

## WHAT KIND OF FIRE?

Chapter 6 presented the biblical teaching that our final destination is a new earth, but it didn't explain how we get from here to there. We learn more from 2 Peter 3:10, which says, "The day of the Lord will come like a thief. The heavens will disappear with a roar; the elements will be destroyed by fire, and the earth and everything done in it will be laid bare." The King James Version ends this verse by saying the earth and its works "shall be burned up."

The popularity of the KJV led generations of English-speaking Christians to assume this world will be annihilated, or "burned up." However, we now have earlier and more reliable Greek manuscripts of this verse that read the earth and its works will be "found." The earth and its works won't be removed. They will be revealed. So the New International Version translates this verse, "The earth and everything done in it will be laid bare," and the English Standard Version says, "The earth and the works that are done on it will be exposed." On the other hand, the latest critical edition of the Greek New Testament surprisingly says, "The earth and the works on it will not be found," which sounds like a vote for annihilation. This reading is controversial because it isn't found in any Greek manuscript, and it signals that this debate will not be resolved soon.[2]

Here is the question: Will this coming fire annihilate the present world, utterly dissolving it like snow on a hot sidewalk? Or will it merely purify the world, as a smelting furnace burns away impurities so that only the pure gold remains? There are compelling reasons to believe it's a purging fire. Peter said the impending fire will destroy the world just as Noah's flood destroyed the world (2 Peter 3:6–7). Those waters did not annihilate the world. They cleansed the world, washing its sin and sinners away. If this is Peter's point of comparison, then it seems likely that the future fire will purge rather than obliterate the world. Peter used the smelting furnace analogy earlier. In 1 Peter 1:7 he explained that trials "have come so that the proven genuineness of your faith — of greater worth than gold, which perishes even though refined by fire — may result in praise, glory and honor when Jesus Christ is revealed."[3]

Besides this biblical evidence, there is a theological argument for a purging rather than annihilating fire. If God were to annihilate this world, he would be conceding something to Satan. He would essentially be saying, "You got me. You messed up my good world so much even I can't get it back. I'm going to have to blow it up and start over somewhere else." I cannot imagine God ever saying that, can you? Everything that sin broke, grace will restore. Satan wins nothing in the end.

> **EVERYTHING THAT SIN BROKE, GRACE WILL RESTORE. SATAN WINS NOTHING IN THE END.**

The New Testament speaks of a "new heaven and a new earth," but it never says there will be a new world (*kosmos*). Instead, it says there is a single world (*kosmos*) with two distinct ages (*aiônes*): the present evil age and the future period of redemption. Jesus assumed this division when he said, "Anyone who speaks against the Holy Spirit will not be forgiven, either in this age or in the age to come" (Matt. 12:32).[4] Bearded prophets in cartoons may wave placards warning THE END IS NEAR, but the Bible never speaks about the end of this world (*kosmos*). Rather, Scripture teaches that our present evil age will give way to a better golden age at the return of Christ. This period of history will end, but not the world itself.

On the other hand, I grant Peter's language is intense. He said, "The heavens will disappear with a roar" and "the elements will melt in the heat" (2 Peter 3:10 – 12 NIV). This may indicate that sin has so permeated creation there won't be much left once the impurities are burned off. Our world may be all but annihilated and replaced with another. This is actually a moot point, because either way, whether by purging or annihilation, we still get to the same place, a new earth. Annihilation wouldn't prevent God from restoring this creation, because the same God who made the world from nothing could re-create it again if he had to. We know he will have to do this for the many dead bodies that have decomposed all the way to nothing. There probably isn't much left of the bodies of the apostles Paul and Peter, yet God will raise them both on the last day. If God will restore annihilated people, he could certainly restore an annihilated world. While I prefer to think the coming fire will merely purify creation, an annihilating fire wouldn't be the end of the world. Really.

## WHAT'S NEW?

Christians may disagree about how we get to the new earth, but they should all agree that Scripture teaches that this is our final destination (Isa. 65:17 – 25; 2 Peter 3:10 – 13; Rev. 21:1 – 5). This raises an important question. The phrase "new earth" implies both continuity and discontinuity with our present world. What is new about the new earth and what stays the same?

We find a hint in 2 Peter 3:13: "But in keeping with his promise we are looking forward to a new heaven and a new earth, where righteousness dwells." Remember our distinction between things and actions? Which category applies to what Peter said about the new earth? The one thing that stands out as new is not a thing at all, but an action. Unlike this present age, which groans beneath the weight of the fall, the new earth is "the home of righteousness" (v. 13 NIV 1984).

There may be a few new things on the new earth — such as new species of animals or flowers — but the Bible doesn't speak about them, and we have good reason to think there won't be. John wrote, "He who was seated on the throne said, 'I am making everything new!' " (Rev. 21:5). Notice God did not say, "I am making new everything!" but rather "I am making everything new!" He does not promise to make new things to furnish the new earth, but to renew the things that are already here. Second-century theologian Irenaeus noticed this and argued that the new earth is substantially identical to this one. He distinguished between things and actions and said it is the "fashion" (see 1 Cor. 7:31; NIV "present form") of this world, not its "substance," that passes away.[5]

This makes good sense of redemption. If redemption restores creation, then its task is not to replace the things of creation but to restore them to their original goodness. The new earth is this earth, only fixed. We often use the term *new* in just this way. When I was in seminary, I owned an old Ford that continually broke down. At one point, the passenger door fell off, so I tied it on with a rope that ran behind the passenger seat to the bottom of mine. Single women can be surprisingly snooty, and many refused to crawl over the driver's seat and stick shift to slide into theirs. So I often drove home from the mechanic, hopelessly alone but happy that my old beater was running again. I even exclaimed, "It's like a new car!" I didn't mean it was a new *thing*, though there may have been a few new parts under the hood. It was the same clunker as before, with the rope looped around the handle of the passenger door, but it was fixed.

NOTICE GOD DID NOT SAY, "I AM MAKING NEW EVERYTHING!" BUT RATHER "I AM MAKING EVERYTHING NEW!"

Or consider the times we feel like "a new person." February in West Michigan can be depressing. After we haven't seen the sun for six or seven weeks, as an early spring tease, a few sun rays will break through for about ten minutes. Immediately we grab a friend and skip around a tree singing, "It's a Small World after All." We giggle and shout, "I feel like a new person!" What do we mean? We haven't changed in our being. We still have the same freckles and hankering for kimchi. We're the same person, just fixed.

Likewise, the new earth is this earth, now fixed. I wouldn't be surprised to find Lake Michigan or Sleeping Bear Dunes on the new earth. Ann Arbor will be gone, because that is part of the fall (said the man from Ohio). The new earth must be very much like this one, for if it is too different from our current version, then it hasn't been redeemed but replaced. Certain aspects may seem dramatically different, but only because our present world is snarled by sin in ways we don't yet comprehend. The new earth will seem different simply because it will be much more like itself.

Redemption restores rather than obliterates creation. Here's a good rule of thumb for deciding what will be on the new earth: If the item in question belongs to creation, expect it to be here. If it belongs to the fall, expect it to be gone. The new earth will likely host every variety of plant and animal. Extinct species will flower and frolic again. Individual people will retain their unique personalities and quirks, now freed from the gnarled perversion of the fall. Disease, scars, and handicaps will be erased forever, lingering only as faint memories that trigger praise for our full salvation.

I only know of three exceptions to this rule. The one good of creation that apparently will not make it through to the new earth is marriage. When the Sadducees tried to trick Jesus by asking about the woman who had eight successive husbands, Jesus replied there won't be marriage in the next life. I suspect this is because of the fall, which opens the door to remarriage through death and divorce. Like some other people, missionary and author Elisabeth Elliot has had three husbands, through no fault of her own. Whom would Elisabeth be married to on the new earth? The fall has so scrambled marriage that God cannot put one marriage back together without violating another. But it's not exactly true that marriage won't exist on the new earth. Marriage between a husband and wife is merely a shadow of the deeper intimacy we all will experience when Jesus returns to marry his bride. We'll all be married — to Jesus (Eph. 5:25 – 32).

Besides this lone good of creation, there are two consequences of the fall that will never be fixed. Isaiah declares that even when the wolf and lamb are feeding together and the lion is eating straw like an ox, yet "dust will be the serpent's food" (Isa. 65:25). God cursed the snake in Eden, and that curse will never be lifted. The other consequence is the scars of Christ. When the resurrected Jesus appeared to his disciples, he went out of his way to show he still bore the scars of his crucifixion (John 20:27).

These permanent effects of the fall will combine to keep us humble. When we've been on the new earth for "ten thousand years, bright shining as the sun," we will never become cocky or think we deserve this. Every time we see a snake slithering in the dust, we will remember the offense of our sin; and every time we see the scarred hands and feet of Jesus, we will remember the price he paid for our salvation. And we'll praise his unfathomable grace.

# CHAPTER 21

# CONSUMMATION

*Narnia will be completely different because it will be much more like itself.*

*Doug Wilson*

Do you remember the Ginsu knife commercials? A Japanese chef demonstrated that even after sawing through a tin can and chopping wood, his fit-for-a-Samurai kitchen knife remained sharp enough to dice tomatoes and slice bread. When the voice-over man asked, "How much would you pay for a knife like this?" you grabbed your checkbook and prepared to write down whatever large number he said next. "But wait! There's more!" the man said, and he threw in a matching carving fork, six-in-one kitchen tool, six precision steak knives, and a spiral slicer — all for $9.95. You bought four.

The consummation is sort of like those old commercials. The story of God would be thrilling enough if it ended with redemption. We'd sell all we had to avoid hell and join God's new creation, and we'd know we had gotten a steal. But wait! There's more! God not only restores creation, he also consummates it. He takes creation to that higher place it was always intended to go. The consummation is redemption plus. The end of God's story is far better than its beginning, in at least five ways.

## ADVANCED CULTURE

God started Adam and Eve in a garden and told them to make something of it, extending Eden's boundaries until the whole unruly world was brought to heel beneath their benevolent rule.

> **THE CONSUMMATION IS REDEMPTION PLUS.**

Their rebellion ruined everything, but it did not stop their progeny from discovering ways to control nature and develop a thriving human culture. The cultural mandate is the one biblical command that our fallen race has kept the best (Gen. 1:28; 2:15). And though we now labor under the sentence of death, it remains true, as Moses prayed, that God will "establish the work of our hands" (Ps. 90:17).

Our works have staying power. When Jesus returns, he will not take out a giant eraser and wipe out several thousand years of human history. He will not send us back into a pristine garden to start from scratch. He will start us out in a well-developed city, the New Jerusalem that descends from heaven. The difference between a garden and a city is culture, so it seems we will enter the new earth with whatever cultural level we have achieved. Some Christians counter that this heavenly city comes from God, so it may be very different from the cities we are building. We should not assume our feeble stabs at culture will participate in God's cosmic renewal. The new earth will include "ships of Tarshish," but this doesn't mean it will also contain your hand-crafted canoe (Isa. 60:9). The wolf and the lamb will lie down together, but we won't speed their reconciliation by starting wolf and lamb ministries (Isa. 65:25).[1]

I agree we should use caution when declaring which of our cultural artifacts will make it through to the new earth. We have a hard enough time preserving Renaissance paintings and Stradivarius violins in this life. What are the odds that any of them will survive the coming fire that will purge the earth? But that makes my point. What one generation passes down to the next is not so much cultural products but cultural know-how. This tree and that house will not survive forever, but the ability to grow healthier trees and build sturdier homes will. Our specific cultural products may not *participate* in God's cosmic renewal, but they do *anticipate* our lives there. On the new earth people "will build houses and dwell in them; they will plant vineyards and eat their fruit" (Isa. 65:21). Where will this knowledge to build better homes and gardens come from? Some of it is being passed along by the magazine of that name.

I don't know whether the Brandenburg Concertos or the Sistine Chapel will make it through to the new earth. It doesn't matter. I expect both Bach and Michelangelo to be there, with nothing but time to create even better works. Imagine what our geniuses will produce when they have forever to experiment and explore without the handicap of sin. Imagine what you will be able to write, build, and play. If you enjoy being human and you enjoy being here, you are going to love the new earth.

Now you can begin to see the terrible lie that many believe about the afterlife. Non-Christians often say they would rather go to hell than heaven because heaven sounds boring and at least they will have their friends in hell. They tragically undersell the destiny of each. The redeemed will not float on clouds, singing round after round of "Shine, Jesus Shine." They will be fully human and fully alive, praising Jesus — yes, because that is what saved humans do — and also enjoying forever the best this redeemed world can offer. Those in hell will endure endless agony as they suffer alone, separated from God, others, and any hope of deliverance. If you want to achieve your human potential, then repent of your sin, the sin that is dragging you to hell, and throw all your weight on Jesus,

> IF YOU ENJOY BEING HUMAN AND YOU ENJOY BEING HERE, YOU ARE GOING TO LOVE THE NEW EARTH.

who came to this earth to cross out your sin and restore the planet.

## SPIRITUAL BODIES

The apostle Paul declared that the resurrection will transform our present "natural" bodies into "spiritual bodies" (1 Cor. 15:42 – 54). He was not saying that our bodies will be nonphysical, because that would deny their resurrection, which requires material bodies to rise and exit their tombs. Our spiritual bodies will be patterned after Jesus' resurrection body, which was pointedly still material (Luke 24:37 – 43). If Jesus is the firstfruits of our resurrection, then we can assume our future bodies will be as physical as his (1 Cor. 15:20).

Gordon Fee observes that the idea of a "spiritual body" would have scandalized the Corinthians, many of whom thought they were spiritual elites who could disregard their bodies, which only weighed down their souls. Paul informed them that they would not achieve full spirituality until their physical resurrection, when they would receive bodies suited to their new life in the Spirit. These spiritual bodies won't be less than physical; they will be more. Fee says these bodies will be spiritual, "not in the sense of 'immaterial' but of 'supernatural,'" for they will be animated by the "life-giving spirit" of "the last Adam," so that they will be unable to die (1 Cor. 15:45).[2]

I list these imperishable bodies with the consummation because they are better than what Adam received in the beginning. Thomas Aquinas explained, "So after the resurrection men will not need food, but in the state of innocence they did."[3] Unlike our present bodies, which begin to break down after a few days without food and water, our resurrection bodies will be guaranteed to live forever. These immortal bodies will enjoy continuous access to the Tree of Life, so we will be doubly protected from death. This is why I'm saving my first bungee jump for the new earth.

An important aside: Whenever I speak on death and resurrection, someone usually asks whether it is okay to use cremation. I say it depends. We're not making God's job impossibly difficult when we choose cremation, because we know he will resurrect millions of people who have died in fires, been digested by animals, or decomposed all the way to nothing. It depends on our motive. We might choose cremation to honor the person. The proper way to dispose of an old flag is not to throw it in the trash but to burn it. Just so, we might cremate our loved one as the ultimate sign of respect. We might also do it to save space (as is common in China) or money (as is common in West Michigan), and this is fine too.

However, we should never choose cremation because we think the body of our loved one is unimportant. Their dead body is not merely the shell that once housed their true self. This is a Platonic, pagan view that I have argued against throughout this book.[4] That body in the casket matters enough to God that he has centered the entire Christian hope upon its resurrection. That body is a vital part of our loved one, and we should handle it as those who plan to see it again.

We should also keep the ashes of our loved one together. When we scatter them across their favorite lake or patch of grass, we are unwisely depicting a pantheistic worldview in which humans are one with nature. We're not. We are uniquely made in the image of God, and we must preserve that honor even in death. When we place their urn in a cemetery or columbarium, we treat our beloved with the dignity that humans deserve. And that place becomes resurrection ground.

## GOD WITH US

In chapter 6, I explained that God is Immanuel—"God with us"—which is the most important way the end of the story surpasses its beginning. God intermittently walked with Adam and Eve in the garden of Eden. He came and left, came and left, but in the end he will come here to stay. Listen to the thrilling conclusion of Scripture: "And I heard a loud voice from the throne saying, 'Look! God's dwelling place is now among the people, and he will dwell with them. They will be his people, and God himself will be with them and be their God'" (Rev. 21:3).

The story of Scripture is the story of Immanuel, because every time God appears he stays here a little bit longer. He comes and goes from Eden. Then he's the pillar and cloud leading the exodus. Next he appears as Jesus — God in tangible, human form. Now he is present invisibly and within us by his Holy Spirit. Finally — can you believe it? — he descends to earth to live with us forever.

This fact of the consummation means the earth is not our problem. One author mistakenly says, "The fact that earth is not our ultimate home explains why, as followers of Jesus, we experience difficulty, sorrow, and rejection in this world."[5] Think about it. Why do we experience difficulty, sorrow, and rejection? Is it because we're in the wrong place? Realtors emphasize location, location, location. Our problem is not location, for we are exactly where God has placed us. Our problem is sin. We experience difficulty, sorrow, and rejection because of the fall. When Jesus returns, he will fix the fall and live forever on this restored planet. This world is good enough for Jesus; it should be plenty good for us.

## GLORIFICATION

When Jesus restores creation, he will confirm us in righteousness so our sin will never ravage this world again. This is another important way the end far exceeds the beginning. Adam and Eve were created with original righteousness but also with the potential to sin. They could not be certain they would never fall, for in fact they did.

Augustine playfully noted that unlike Adam and Eve, who were merely *posse peccare* (*able not to sin*), glorified humans will be *non posse peccare* (*not able to sin*). This belief in our continued state of glory is grounded in such texts as 1 Peter 5:4: "When the Chief Shepherd appears, you will receive the crown of glory that will never fade away"; and Romans 8:29–30: God "predestined [some] to be conformed to the image of his Son," and "those he predestined, he also called; those he called, he also justified; those he justified, he also glorified."

Consider this special joy of the new earth: We will live forever in loving community with God and each other, with the peace of mind that comes from the absolute certainty that God will not allow us to mess this up.

> WE WILL LIVE FOREVER IN LOVING COMMUNITY WITH GOD AND EACH OTHER, WITH THE PEACE OF MIND THAT COMES FROM THE ABSOLUTE CERTAINTY THAT GOD WILL NOT ALLOW US TO MESS THIS UP.

## BETTER UNDERSTANDING OF GOD

There is one extra of the consummation that is better not despite our fall but because of it. Adam and Eve knew God was good, but they never could have guessed the depth of his love until they had rebelled and been restored. Forgiven sinners like us understand the grace of God even better than the angels, who stand on tiptoe to peer into the gospel, trying to make sense of it (1 Peter 1:12). The angels have never needed the grace of salvation, and they can only puzzle at the patient mercy of God that we know by experience.

Our forgiveness naturally fills us with gratitude, which as any counselor can tell you, is a necessary ingredient for joy. The consummation is a large part of the answer to our question, "Can you serve Jesus and still enjoy your life?" Your life may be excruciatingly difficult, but stop and think about the many mores God has promised you: everlasting life in his presence, here on earth, enveloped in an embrace of love that forgives every sin you've ever done, enjoying ever-escalating cultural breakthroughs with the assurance that nothing will ever go wrong again. Do you feel a first wave of gratitude? It brings the rising tide of joy.

# CHAPTER 22

# WHAT NOW?

Life is meant to be spent.

*N. D. Wilson*

**C**an you serve Jesus and still enjoy your life? Originally Mennonite and raised Baptist, I come from a long tradition of defying worldliness. My fondest memories include my junior high Sunday school teacher, Mr. Mills, earnestly imploring us to resist the evil trinity of the world, the flesh, and the Devil, and pretty much in that order.

A health food aficionado before organic was cool, this trim, elderly gentleman championed all foods natural. My friends and I found his eccentric passion far more interesting than relearning another Bible story, and we often interrupted his lesson with queries about the nutritional value of our Sunday dinners. These questions were impossible for Mr. Mills to resist. Each time he patiently explained how our mothers were poisoning our young bodies with processed food, especially those chemicals and preservatives found in taco sauce. This last comment elicited howls of laughter from the other boys, because everyone knew the Wittmers religiously ate tacos every Sunday (though not for religious reasons; we just happened to like them).

When Mr. Mills wasn't scaring us with the odds of contracting cancer from our worldly diet, he was quietly warning us about the spiritual dangers of worldliness. He referred often to James 4:4, "Don't you know that friendship with the world is hatred toward God? Anyone who chooses to be a friend of the world becomes an enemy of God" (NIV 1984). One of his favorite lines was that Christians who had *assurance* did not need *insurance.* People only buy insurance when they no longer trust God to protect them from the world (though given what he knew we were eating, health insurance probably did not sound like a bad idea).

The worship service that followed was another poignant reminder that we were different from the world. Our pastor repeated John's counsel that since we were "not of the world," we must not "love the world or anything in the world" (John 17:14; 1 John 2:15). Rather, we should brace ourselves for the impending "trouble" and "persecution" that the world's "hatred" would soon heap on us (John 16:33; 15:18 – 20). He illustrated the point by warning that our state's Department of Social Services was starting to remove children from Christian homes. I fought back tears and wondered how long it would be until the authorities came for us.

In response to our pastor's stirring sermons, we bravely sang that "earthly pleasures vainly call me" and "nothing worldly shall enthrall me," for "I would be like Jesus."[1] And though "the world is ever near," with "tempting sounds" and "sights that dazzle,"[2] we would seek "to live above the world" and set our hearts on "higher ground."[3] We confessed we were nothing more than a "stranger on earth, a sinner by choice and an alien by birth."[4] We could hardly wait until "the roll is called up yonder" and we are gathered to our "home beyond the skies,"[5] where, except for "pearly gates" and "streets of gold,"[6] we knew almost nothing about our "flight to worlds unknown."[7] We were "marching to Zion," "to fairer worlds on high,"[8] "to a home on God's celestial shore,"[9] and we couldn't care less about "the pleasures earthly things afford."[10]

Except that we did.

*Can you serve Jesus and still enjoy your life?*

My childhood overflowed with an embarrassing number of simple, earthly pleasures. My family routinely hosted whiffle ball and kick ball games for the neighborhood — saint and sinner alike. We doubled over with laughter when a mom next door struck out an intensely competitive guy or when an overzealous base runner slipped on the dewy grass rounding third. We played deep into the night. When lengthening shadows made it too dangerous to continue, we simply switched games to hide-and-seek or kick the can. We went to bed weary and with wide smiles.

My brothers and I enjoyed the same worldly pleasures as other boys. We played Little League baseball, traded baseball cards, bought a pony, rode bikes, even sold lemonade. We went on fishing trips to Canada, where monster bluegills sent shockwaves up our poles and through our hands as they dove for cover. Every evening ended the same perfect way, with our family sitting under the stars, dining on fresh fish and hushpuppies and swapping stories and laughter until the swarming mosquitoes drove us to our beds.

Our Mennonite heritage did not make us Amish, so we watched a bit of television, especially *Happy Days*, *CHiPs*, and the *Dukes of Hazzard*. We pretended we were Fonzie, Ponch, and the Duke boys, driving fast cycles and cars with fast women. I once ate a mouthful of gravel when, in imitation of the Fonz jumping the shark, I turned my handlebars to the right while in midair and quickly learned it's best for both wheels to point in the same direction when contact is resumed with the ground. Occasionally we snuck in an episode of *Love Boat* when our parents were away, but we never watched *Dallas*. We weren't that worldly.

We also spent much time — way too much, in retrospect — cheering for every Cleveland sports team. And though every season ends in frustration, with vague plans and high draft choices for next year, my brothers and I still care far more than we should. Win or usually lose, we could always count on mom's comfort food. Her Mennonite meals — sandwiches made from homemade bread, trail bologna, and Swiss cheese, were the envy of the cafeteria. My classmates often stole my lunch, or, if that was unsuccessful, would beg to trade their sorry store-bought snacks for my homemade apple, blueberry, and whoopee pies (if you don't know what those are, you can be sure your childhood was not as happy as mine).

> **WE WEREN'T UNSPIRITUAL. WE WERE SAINTS, AND THE VERY BEST KIND. WE WERE WORLDLY SAINTS.**

Despite our churchly protests, we were fairly consumed with the earthly pleasures of this world. We could sing to our hearts' content about the transitory and tempting nature of the world, but in fact our hearts were most content when we were most involved with the happiness we found here. We weren't unspiritual. We were saints, and the very best kind. We were worldly saints.

*Can you serve Jesus and still enjoy your life?*

By now you know my answer to this question. It starts with your call and ends with it too. *Do whatever God is calling you to do, no more and no less. Do it with all your might; then go to bed.* Your life will count for eternity, and you'll probably even like it. But how can you tell whether you are answering God's call? Here are three keys, suspiciously alliterated: critique, charity, and contentment.

## CRITIQUE

During peacetime, people settle into a routine. They go to work, raise a family, and take vacations as people have done for thousands of years. Not when they're living in a war zone. Then they hunker in bunkers and do whatever it takes to defeat the enemy that threatens their lives. This is what makes the global war on terror so confusing. We have an enemy that seeks to destroy us, yet it hides in the shadows and only strikes when we're not paying attention. So we remain vigilant, all the while going about our business as if life was normal. When we avoid large crowds or significantly change our routines, the terrorists win.

Satan was kicked out of heaven when he stood toe-to-toe with God, and ever since he has resorted to terrorist tactics. He embodied trusted creatures, a serpent and Judas, to deceive God's people and blow up God's works of creation and redemption. God declared war on Satan's terrorism, which puts us in an awkward spot. We must live in creation as God originally intended, doing meaningful work, loving our families and friends, and making space to savor the many gifts of his world. But the pleasures of creation must not lull us to sleep. We are at war, and we must never forget our heavenly calling to "put on the full armor of God, so that you can take your stand against the Devil's schemes. For our struggle is not against flesh and blood, but against the rulers, against the authorities, against the powers of this dark world and against the spiritual forces of evil in the heavenly realms" (Eph. 6:11 – 12).

There is no one-size-fits-all playbook for how to live during a war on terror. Some people are called to lead the charge against terrorism, while others are called to keep the normal flow of life going. If all run to one side or the other, our ship will tip and the terrorists will win. Whatever our calling in the kingdom of God, we all should feel the pinch of promoting the heavenly purpose of redemption while enjoying the earthly pleasures of creation. We must continually assess how we're doing on both counts. How long

IF WE EVER STOP FEELING THE PULL BETWEEN CREATION AND REDEMPTION, THAT CAN ONLY MEAN WE'VE FALLEN OFF ONE SIDE OR THE OTHER.

has it been since we spoke to someone about Jesus? How long since we prayed for just this opportunity? Do we look for ways to leverage our resources for the kingdom, or do we find excuses to give less? What have we sacrificed for our Lord?

But our passion for redemption will distort the gospel if it leads us to neglect creation. So we must also ask whether we're getting enough sleep and exercise. What do we do for fun? How long since we splurged on the people we love? Are we fully present when we are with them? Do they know we love them as ends, not merely as means to some higher spiritual goal? What normal, earthly needs are begging for our attention?

Be glad for the tension these questions generate. If we ever stop feeling the pull between creation and redemption, that can only mean we've fallen off one side or the other. Still, these questions can be overwhelming, so it's important to extend charity both to ourselves and to others.

## CHARITY

When I was in college, my church conducted a building campaign. I had an extra $2,000 in my savings account, and I decided to give all of it. I didn't need the money to get through school, as tuition was still low in those days and I could pay my way by scholarships and summer work. I don't remember if I followed through with that initial commitment, but I'm still amazed at the generosity of my younger self. I would not be so quick to empty my savings account today, mostly because I have a family that depends on me. Any extra $2,000 that comes in could easily be spent on property taxes; college funds; retirement accounts; or life, homeowners, automobile, and umbrella insurance.

Now that I think about it, the only reason my younger self could consider giving away two grand is because my parents were paying the property taxes and insurance on my home. Do not overlook the value of ordinary callings. Praise God for the widow who gave her last mite, and praise God for the foundational faithfulness of others that makes such extraordinary sacrifice possible.

Be slow to judge and quick to give others the benefit of the doubt. Don't immediately criticize pastors and missionaries who leave the ministry to sell houses or insurance, thinking they have settled for less than God's best. Many ordination councils include the solemn warning, "Young man, if you can do anything else than pastor, you should do it. Only enter the ministry if you wouldn't be happy doing anything else." I understand what the speaker is trying to communicate, but I have always thought that is an odd way to put it. Don't we want pastors with a wide range of gifts and interests? If a person really can't do anything else, I'm not sure I want to give that person charge of my soul.

If our pastors are curious and talented people, it shouldn't surprise us that after twenty or thirty years they might want to try their hand at something else. They aren't necessarily sinning when they leave the ministry. In fact, they will have many more evangelistic opportunities as a real estate or insurance agent than they ever did as a pastor. Let's not fret about the callings of others. As Jesus told Peter when he obsessed over John, "If I want him to remain alive until I return, what is that to you? You must follow me" (John 21:22).

## CONTENTMENT

Besides the need to critique our values and extend grace to others, we can be confident we have embraced God's call when we don't worry about our success. Many Christians feel enormous pressure to do something great for God. An ordinary life might be good enough for normal people, but they want to step out in faith, challenge God's power, and change the world! When the money doesn't come in, their book doesn't become a bestseller, and their ministry isn't noted in *Christianity Today*, they begin to wonder whether they have failed. Or worse, *are failures*.

The most liberating day in my professional life was when I realized I am only responsible to answer God's call. I am not responsible for what comes of it. It doesn't matter whether I am slave or free, rich or poor, the focus of every room or largely forgotten, I please God whenever I do what God has called me to do (1 Cor. 7:17 – 24). Results may vary, and that's okay. I am complete in Christ. My identity is settled in him. Everything else is gravy (Col. 2:9 – 10).

I recently preached on our Christian vocation, and afterward a young man asked if he might be allowed to change callings to something he wasn't as good at but might enjoy more. He feared this might doom him to being less successful than he might otherwise be, but he was weary of the people and pressures of his current job. Would God be okay with him trying something else?

I told him about my professor Richard Muller, a world-class church historian who would soon retire, in part so he could oil paint. Dr. Muller is a fine artist, but he is an even better theologian, so in one sense it seems a shame for him to retire at the top of his game. And yet there is no rule that says he must teach theology and supervise dissertations until they wheel him out in a box. He has faithfully served God in decades of teaching ministry, and he will continue to serve God as he paints Dutch landscapes. Before someone accuses Dr. Muller of wasting his retirement, remember that he will continue to research and write, just at a more leisurely pace. He hopes to be even more productive, once he is released from his regular teaching load.

I told the man that his larger need, as is mine, is to find his identity in Christ. Who we are is who we are in Christ. Period. We can't make ourselves any more valuable, or any less. Our value is fixed in Jesus, which frees us both to succeed and to fail. We can succeed without fretting about maintaining our momentum, because our accomplishments have not changed our value one bit. We're also free to fail, for the very same reason. Who we are is a gift we receive, not a task we must achieve. So yes, my friend is free to change careers, but it will not significantly improve his joy unless he finds his joy in Christ.

> WHO WE ARE IS A GIFT WE RECEIVE, NOT A TASK WE MUST ACHIEVE.

Can you serve Jesus and still enjoy your life?

You tell me, and put it in the form of a story. Start with creation and run clear through to the consummation, and you'll know that not only is it possible to enjoy your life while serving Jesus, but it's the only way you can.

APPENDIX

# PARTIAL FALL?

> But if the cosmos in its present condition is *abnormal*,
> then a *disturbance* has taken place in the past, and only
> a *regenerating* power can warrant it the final attainment
> of its goal.
>
> *Abraham Kuyper*

The insurmountable problems with denying a literal Adam and a historical fall, together with their commitment to God's Word, persuade most evangelical theologians to follow Scripture's teaching that Adam's sin is responsible for the mess we are in. However, some are equally persuaded by modern science's belief that death is natural, and they wonder if physical death might be a normal part of creation, even for humans.

In his commentary on Romans 5:12 – 21, N. T. Wright says Adam and Eve might have died even if they had never sinned. He writes, "All that lived in God's original world would decay and perish, but 'death' in that sense carried no sting." When God warned them they would die if they ate from the forbidden tree, he was referring to spiritual death, "a darker force, opposed to creation itself, unmaking that which was good, always threatening to drag the world back toward chaos." So "when humans turned away in sin from the creator … what might have been a natural sleep acquired a sense of shame and threat."[1] Thomas Long agrees with this distinction between physical and spiritual death, and he uses lowercase "death" for the physical death that is natural for humans and uppercase "Death" for the spiritual death that is the consequence of sin.[2]

I think this separation of physical and spiritual death, if carried through to its logical end, will destroy the Christian faith. Paul said that God "has reconciled you by Christ's physical body through death to present you holy in his sight" (Col. 1:22). But if we separate physical from spiritual death, how can the physical death of Jesus bring us spiritual life? Furthermore, if physical death is normal and only spiritual death is the enemy, it seems likely that Jesus only spiritually rose from the dead. And then, as Paul told the Corinthians, we are still in our sins (1 Cor. 15:17). If Adam's sin brought only spiritual death, why wouldn't the Last Adam's obedience bring only a kind of spiritual life? If physical death is the natural way of the world, even for humans, then perhaps there is no bodily resurrection, but merely a spiritual peace that God supplies in the midst of our extinction.

**IF GOD MADE OUR BODIES TO DIE BEFORE SIN ENTERED THE WORLD, WHY WOULD WE TRUST HIM TO GRANT US EVERLASTING LIFE AFTERWARD?**

Redemption restores creation to its original goodness (Acts 3:21; Eph. 1:10; Col. 1:20). But if this original goodness contained human death, what hope do we have of everlasting life? Someone might argue that everlasting life is part of the consummation; it's an important way that the end is better than the beginning. While it's true that our future "spiritual body" will transcend our present "natural body" (1 Cor. 15:42–49), Scripture also teaches that our natural body is God's good gift that only dies because of sin (Rom. 5:12; 1 Cor. 15:21–22; 1 Tim. 4:1–6). If God made our bodies to die before sin entered the world, why would we trust him to grant us ever-lasting life afterward?

Some theologians brush these problems aside and insist that physical death is natural for humans because we are inherently mortal. Adam and Eve would have died without access to the Tree of Life, so obviously it is natural for us to die. I agree that Adam and Eve could not sustain their lives on their own steam. They needed to eat from the Tree of Life, but they lost this access when they sinned. The *possibility* of death is always present with finite creatures (we have everlasting life because God sustains us, not because we are inherently immortal), but the *actuality* of human death is a consequence of sin.[3]

Abraham Kuyper argued that rather than capitulate to the claims of evolutionary science, it was necessary to push back. He said there are two kinds of scientists, normalists and abnormalists. Normalists believe the world has evolved gradually in unbroken succession from previous life forms, so whatever exists now is normal. It is normal for lions to pounce on the back of water buffalo, twig beetles to inject a fungus that kills black walnut trees, and everything, including humans, to wear out and die. Normalists can't make ultimate sense of the world because they are looking at the scene of an accident without knowing there has been an accident. They think the buckled fenders and bodies strewn across the road are normal. They don't even know what they're looking at.[4]

Abnormalists are in a much better position because they recognize a catastrophic fall has occurred, so that much of what we see is not the way it is supposed to be. This doesn't answer all of our questions, as we still must wrestle with such findings as the presence of incisors in the fossil record. We won't hold our hands over our ears and shut our minds, but neither will we let scientists tell us which parts of the Bible we are allowed to believe. We will humbly push back, saying that the cataclysmic fall and flood should influence how we read the data of nature, just as the findings of science can help us to better read Scripture.

We may not solve every question, but we stake our lives on the biblical teaching that Adam's fall devastated God's good world. This turns out to be good news, because if the fall is an unnatural interruption, there is hope that God can do something about it. And we believe he already has.

# DISCUSSION QUESTIONS

## Chapter 1: Heaven and Earth

1. When have you felt the tension between serving Jesus and enjoying life?
2. What choice did you make in that situation? Did you resolve the tension in favor of Jesus, enjoyment, or both?
3. How might it improve both our lives and success at sharing the gospel if we could better answer this question?

## Chapter 2: Fables

1. How have your thoughts and actions been influenced by our culture's dominant belief in naturalism?
2. How have your thoughts and actions been influenced by the church's fixation on an immaterial heaven?
3. Are you most inclined to make the mistake of naturalism or spiritualism?

## Chapter 3: One Story

1. How would you define human flourishing? How can you tell whether you are flourishing?

2. What area of your life must you liberate from the overly "spiritual" expectations of yourself or others? Why is this hard?

3. What area of your life must you still submit to the lordship of Christ? Why is this hard?

## CHAPTER 4: TWO DISTINCTIONS

1. How does our natural/supernatural distinction differ from Plato's division between heaven and earth and between the human soul and body?

2. Why is God's judgment the only thing that gives ultimate meaning to life?

3. Where do you experience the tension between creation and redemption? Give one example and describe how you navigate the tension.

## CHAPTER 5: IT'S ALL GOOD

1. Why is the goodness of creation an essential foundation for the gospel?

2. Does Jesus still possess his human soul and body? Why might this matter?

3. How does the Christian belief in the resurrection of the body differ from the Platonic belief in the immortality of the soul? Why is this difference important?

## CHAPTER 6: YOU ARE ALREADY HOME

1. Can you think of examples from songs, books, or sermons that present too low a view of creation?

2. How might the location of our home (heaven or earth) change how we live?

3. How often do you pray for the kingdom to come? Why don't we long for it more?

## CHAPTER 7: RIGHTLY DIVIDING THE WORD

1. How does the distinction between thing and action help you to better understand the Bible? What remaining questions do you have?
2. How does the distinction between thing and action help you to integrate your human and Christian life? What remaining questions do you have?
3. How does the distinction between thing and action raise the bar for our Christian lives? How might it imply that God expects more from us rather than less?

## CHAPTER 8: WHERE DO YOU ENJOY GOD'S WORLD?

1. Why is it important for Christians to enjoy their earthly lives? What do we lose when we forget to be human?
2. What do we risk when we make too much of creation? What do we risk when we make too little of creation?
3. Which tendency is a greater temptation for you?

## CHAPTER 9: LOVE GOD

1. How does the distinction between thing and action enable us to distinguish between a good and bad meaning of the term *worldly*?
2. What are the two ways to become worldly (in the sinful sense of that word)? Which way do you most need to watch out for?
3. Why is it essential to remember that both our body and soul belong entirely to the realm of nature? Why is it also essential to remember that we natural creatures have a supernatural goal?

## CHAPTER 10: SERVE OTHERS

1. Why are personal relationships the foundation of our happiness and success?
2. Why is it necessary for us and for the world that God is triune? What would we lose if God were merely a single person rather than three persons in one essence?
3. Whom do you need to serve better? How might the commands and example of Jesus inspire you to do this?

## CHAPTER 11: CULTIVATE THE EARTH

1. List all your callings that you can think of. Which ones are most important? Are you giving them the attention they deserve?
2. How does the gospel free you to enjoy and excel in your callings?
3. Consider the place where you work. What product or service does your business provide? How does your job serve others within your company? Why is it important to answer both questions?

## CHAPTER 12: REST EVERY SEVENTH DAY

1. How does the Sabbath teach us that creation and redemption complement rather than merely compete with each other?
2. Are you in the habit of taking a Sabbath rest? Why or why not? Is your reason acceptable to God?
3. Do you think of the Sabbath as a rule to follow or as a gift from God? How might you enjoy a Sabbath rest without falling into legalism?

## CHAPTER 13: WHAT IS YOUR CALL?

1. Why is it important to do your current callings with all your might, as for the Lord? Are you performing them well enough to earn God's reward?
2. Is being a pastor or missionary a higher calling than selling shoes? Why or why not?

3. Is God calling you to change your vocation? How would you know?

## CHAPTER 14: THE FALL THEN AND NOW

1. Why must Christians believe that the fall happened? What do we lose if there wasn't a historical Adam who ruined an originally good creation with his rebellion?
2. What prevents us from creating the perfect church or family? Why will we never stop fighting the fall?
3. Where do you see autonomy in your life? When is it easier to spot?

## CHAPTER 15: THE FALLOUT FROM THE FALL

1. Why is it essential to remember that death is our enemy? What do we lose if we suggest that death is a good thing?
2. Where do you most clearly see the effects of sin in your world? What are you doing about it? What can you do about it?
3. Why is the doctrine of hell essential for understanding Jesus' death on the cross?

## CHAPTER 16: HOW DO YOU FIGHT THE FALL?

1. What ethical question do you need to evaluate through the grid of creation, fall, and redemption? Draw three columns on a sheet of paper and make your lists.
2. How might focusing on the goodness of creation encourage you to avoid the sins of the fall? What specific temptation would this method help you to conquer?
3. Why is it unthinkable for Christians to entertain themselves with sin?

## CHAPTER 17: GOSPEL

1. How would you define the gospel?

2. How does your understanding of the gospel change the way you live? What response does it call from you?

3. What words do you use to describe sin? Do these words sufficiently convey sin's deserved misery?

## CHAPTER 18: KINGDOM

1. How can you follow Jesus right where you are? What is Jesus calling you to do today?

2. What is your role in your local church, and how is this different from your role in your culture? How might these two roles reinforce rather than compete with each other?

3. Why must the gathered church focus on the Word and the scattered church focus on deeds? What happens when we switch this focus?

## CHAPTER 19: ALREADY BUT NOT YET

1. Why is it important to say that the kingdom is already here but not yet in its fullness? What do we miss if we omit either one?

2. Why must we say that everything matters but some things matter more than others? What do we lose if we omit either part?

3. Are you serving the kingdom when you prepare venison for your church's wild game dinner evangelistic outreach? Are you still serving the kingdom when you share the leftover venison with a neighbor? Is there a difference? Why or why not?

## CHAPTER 20: NEW EARTH

1. Do you think the coming fire will utterly annihilate or merely purge this earth? Why or why not does this matter?

2. What excites you most about the new earth? What are you most looking forward to?

3. What questions do you still have about the new earth?

## CHAPTER 21: CONSUMMATION

1. Given the thrilling vision of the new earth, what would you say to someone who says they would rather go to hell than heaven because heaven sounds boring?
2. What are you doing today that anticipates your life on the new earth?
3. What does it say about God that the end of his story is even better than its good beginning?

## CHAPTER 22: WHAT NOW?

1. How are childhoods today different from yours? How might you encourage children to enjoy God's world?
2. How does thinking of sin as acts of terrorism inform the tension we feel between creation and redemption? Why is there no one-size-fits-all answer for how to respond?
3. Why is discerning our call the key to navigating the tension between the earthly pleasures of creation and the heavenly purpose of redemption? How does your call simultaneously challenge you to do more and leave you content with your level of success?

## APPENDIX: PARTIAL FALL?

1. Romans 5:12–21 declares that human death is a result of Adam's fall, but what about animal death? What reasons do we have for thinking animal death is a consequence of Adam's sin? What reasons do we have for thinking it isn't?
2. How might the separation of physical and spiritual death indicate a Platonic view of the world?
3. What recent challenges have you heard to Scripture's teaching about sin and death? How did you answer them?

# ACKNOWLEDGMENTS

I am thankful for the many students and church groups who patiently listened and pushed back as I taught this material over the past decade. Their penetrating questions helped refine these thoughts and, most importantly, led back to the Scriptures. The story of creation, fall, and redemption may be inspiring, but we're wasting our time if it isn't what God's Word teaches.

I also received valuable insights from my editors, Ryan Pazdur, Jim Ruark, and Andy Jones; my wife, Julie; and my friends Jonathan Shelley, Kevin Heyne, Ted McCully, Matthew Westerholm, and Steve Dye. Their suggestions have made this a better book. I've scrubbed the manuscript for errors many times and am happy to report now that there aren't any. In the unlikely event that you find one, or several, they're on me.

# NOTES

## Chapter 1: Heaven and Earth

1. Billy Joel, "Only the Good Die Young," on *The Stranger* album (Columbia, 1977).
2. Billy Joel, "My Life," on *52nd Street* album (Columbia, 1978).
3. David Platt, *Radical Together* (Colorado Springs: Multnomah, 2011), 15–19.
4. This point is well argued in Larry Osborne, *Accidental Pharisees* (Grand Rapids: Zondervan, 2012), 90–94, 167–69, 187–89.
5. Ron Sider, *Rich Christians in an Age of Hunger* (Dallas: Word, 1990), 153.

## Chapter 2: Fables

1. C. S. Lewis, "The Funeral of a Great Myth," in *Christian Reflections*, ed. Walter Hooper (1967; repr., Grand Rapids: Eerdmans, 1989), 86–88, 93.
2. Not all naturalists are materialists, as some who deny the possibility of supernatural intervention nevertheless believe that immaterial elements comprise part of the natural order. However, since materialism is the dominant form of naturalism, I have restricted my focus to this variety. See Ronald H. Nash, *Life's Ultimate Questions* (Grand Rapids: Zondervan, 1999), 37–38; and Alvin Plantinga, "Against Naturalism," in Alvin Plantinga and Michael Tooley, *Knowledge of God* (Malden, MA: Blackwell, 2008), 31–33, 49–51.
3. For example, see John Calvin, *Institutes of the Christian Religion* 1.15.2, ed. John T. McNeill, trans. Ford Lewis Battles (Philadelphia: Westminster, 1960), 184, 186; and "Psychopannychia," in *Calvin's Tracts*, trans. Henry Beveridge (Edinburgh: Calvin Translation Society, 1851), 3:442–43.

## Chapter 3: One Story

1. m-w.com, s.v. "flourish," *http://www.merriam-webster.com/dictionary/flourish*.
2. Abraham Kuyper, "Souvereiniteit in Eigen Kring," in *Abraham Kuyper: A Centennial Reader*, trans. and ed. James D. Bratt (Grand Rapids: Eerdmans, 1998), 488 (emphasis Kuyper's).

## CHAPTER 4: TWO DISTINCTIONS

1. Gerard Manley Hopkins, "The Principle or Foundation," in *Gerard Manley Hopkins: The Major Works*, ed. Catherine Phillips (New York: Oxford University Press, 2002), 292.
2. I am paraphrasing a line from John Piper, who said something similar in a sermon at Lausanne III: "We Christians care about all human suffering, especially eternal suffering." Cited in Justin Taylor, "We Care about All Suffering in This Age—Especially Eternal Suffering," *Between Two Worlds* (November 18, 2010), *http://thegospelcoalition.org/blogs/justintaylor/2010/11/18/we-care-about-all-suffering-in-this-age%E2%80%94especially-eternal-suffering/*.

## CHAPTER 5: IT'S ALL GOOD

1. Like many other medieval artists and theologians, Michelangelo was a Neoplatonist who referred to the human body as an "earthly prison." See Deborah Walker, *Michelangelo and the Art of Letter Writing* (Cambridge: Cambridge University Press, 2010), 87–89, 111–15.
2. Gregory of Nazianzus, Epistle CI.184A, in J. Stevenson, ed. *Creeds, Councils and Controversies*, rev. W. H. C. Frend (London: SPCK, 1989), 90.
3. Irenaeus, *Against Heresies* III.4, in J. Stevenson, ed. *A New Eusebius*, rev. W. H. C. Frend (London: SPCK, 1987), 116.
4. Ibid. Marcion is significant because he created his own Bible, which prompted the church to consider which books belonged in its canon. Marcion eliminated the entire Old Testament and any allusions to it in the New Testament. This left him with only a mutilated edition of Luke and ten of Paul's epistles, with any reference to the Law or creation cut out.
5. Rick Osborne and Ed Strauss, *Bible Angels and Demons* (Grand Rapids: ZonderKidz, 2004), 6.
6. "Poll Reveals Few Believe in Physical Resurrection," *Grand Rapids Press* (April 8, 2006), D9.

## CHAPTER 6: YOU ARE ALREADY HOME

1. Isaiah uses the plural, "new heavens and a new earth."
2. William W. Walford, "Sweet Hour of Prayer," 1845, public domain (emphasis added).
3. Harriet E. Buell, "A Child of the King," 1877, public domain (emphasis added).
4. James M. Black, "When the Roll Is Called Up Yonder," 1892, public domain (emphasis added).
5. George Atkins, "Brethren, We Have Met to Worship," nineteenth century, public domain (emphasis added).
6. "Temporary Home," by Luke Robert Laird, Zachary David Maloy, and Carrie Underwood, lyrics copyright © Universal Music Publishing Group.

## CHAPTER 7: RIGHTLY DIVIDING THE WORD

1. The most precise way to express this distinction is with the terms *ontology* (the study of being) and *ethics* (the study of morality), but "things versus actions"

roughly represents the ontological/ethical distinction and is more easily understood by a general audience.

2. It is important to grasp this distinction between thing and action, noun and verb, or ontology and ethics, because the New Testament uses *kosmos*, its most popular term for "world," in both ways. Ontologically, *kosmos* offers a telescoping array of ever-tightening definitions. In its broadest sense, *kosmos* signifies the entire created universe, as in Paul's declaration in Athens that God "made the world and everything in it" (Acts 17:24). Often it is used more specifically to indicate only the inhabited part of this universe, or planet Earth, as in Satan's offer to give Jesus "all the kingdoms of the world" in return for his worship (Matt. 4:8). And even more narrowly, *kosmos* can represent the people who live on this planet, as in the Pharisees' lament that "the whole world has gone after" Jesus (John 12:19).

   Unfortunately, the crowd's enthusiasm for Jesus soon waned and they decided to kill him. This is why the New Testament often uses *kosmos* in an ethical sense, to represent those people who reject Christ and the sinful culture they create (John 7:7; 8:23; 12:31; 14:17; 15:18–19; 16:8, 33; 17:14, 16; 18:36; Rom. 3:6, 19; 1 Cor. 1:20–21; 2:12; 3:19; 5:10; 11:32; 2 Cor. 7:10; Gal. 4:3; Eph. 2:2; Col. 2:8, 20; James 1:27; 4:4; 1 John 2:2, 15–17; 3:1, 13; 4:5; 5:4). Jesus warned his disciples that the same world that hated him would also hate them, for he came to judge the world and drive out its evil prince (John 15:18–19; 12:31).

3. Martin Luther, "Fourth Sermon at Wittenberg," in *Luther's Works*, gen. ed. Helmut T. Lehman, ed. and trans. John W. Doberstein (Philadelphia: Muhlenberg, 1959), 51:85.

4. Rick Warren, *The Purpose Driven Life* (Grand Rapids: Zondervan, 2002), 49.

5. Ibid., 51 (emphasis his).

## CHAPTER 8: WHERE DO YOU ENJOY GOD'S WORLD?

1. John Calvin, *Institutes of the Christian Religion* 1.11.8, ed. John T. McNeill, trans. Ford Lewis Battles (Philadelphia: Westminster, 1960), 108.

2. Jonathan Edwards, "The End for Which God Created the World," in John Piper, *God's Passion for His Glory* (Wheaton: Crossway, 1998), 158.

3. I borrowed some ideas from Doug Wilson for the previous paragraph as well. For these as well as this quote see Doug Wilson, "The Barkity Midnight Dog," *Blog & Mablog* (May 14, 2010), *http://dougwils.com/?s=a+full+tank+of+gas* and *http://dougwils.com/s7-engaging-the-culture/the-barkity-barkity-midnight-dog.html*.

4. Dan Hicks, "How Can I Miss You When You Won't Go Away?"

5. For a succinct summary of Edwards's view, including the source of these quotes, see John W. Cooper, *Panentheism: The Other God of the Philosophers* (Grand Rapids: Baker Academic, 2006), 74–77. Edwards's panentheism seems evident in his view of what happens in heaven. In Miscellany #5 he wrote, "As [the holiest of all] see further into the divine perfections than others, so they shall penetrate further into the vast and infinite distance that is between them

and God, and *their delight of annihilating themselves, that God may be all in all, shall be the greater."* See Piper, *God's Passion for His Glory*, 161 (emphasis mine).

## PART 2: THE MEANING OF LIFE

1. Rick Warren, *The Purpose Driven Life* (Grand Rapids: Zondervan, 2002), 306. Warren explicitly limits his five purposes to Christian activities, concluding, "A great commitment to the Great Commandment and the Great Commission will make you a great Christian."
2. C. S. Lewis, "Learning in War-Time," in *The Weight of Glory* (San Francisco: Harper San Francisco, 1980), 51.

## CHAPTER 9: LOVE GOD

1. Daniel Schorn, "Tom Brady: The Winner," *CBSNews.com* (November 3, 2005), *http://www.cbsnews.com/2100-18560_162-1008148-3.html?pageNum=3&tag =contentMain;contentBody*.
2. Augustine, *Confessions* I.1, trans. Henry Chadwick (New York: Oxford University Press, 1991), 3.
3. Helen H. Lemmel, "Turn Your Eyes upon Jesus" (1922).

## CHAPTER 10: SERVE OTHERS

1. Millard Erickson asserts that God is "not merely selfish," but he seeks his own glory in part to preserve "the nature of things." See Millard Erickson, *God the Father Almighty* (Grand Rapids: Baker, 1998), 246. Jonathan Edwards and John Piper argue that while some might pejoratively say God is selfish or narcissistic to delight in himself above all things, it is precisely this infinite love for himself that supplies the possibility of happiness to humans. See John Piper, *God's Passion for His Glory* (Wheaton: Crossway, 1998), 152, 168–70.
2. I learned to describe the Trinity as "a community of self-giving lovers" from Cornelius Plantinga Jr. See also Arthur C. McGill, *Suffering: A Test of Theological Method* (Philadelphia: Westminster, 1982), 53–82.
3. Quoted by Joshua Wolf Shenk, "What Makes Us Happy?" *The Atlantic* (June 1, 2009), *http://www.theatlantic.com/magazine/archive/2009/06/what-makes-us -happy/307439/?single_page=true*.
4. Michael Reeves, *Delighting in the Trinity* (Downers Grove, IL: IVP Academic, 2012), 52–56.
5. *The Gospel of Thomas*, Logion 114, in J. M. Robinson, ed., *The Nag Hammadi Library*, 3rd ed. (San Francisco: Harper & Row, 1988), 138. For a fuller discussion, see Reeves, *Delighting in the Trinity*.

## CHAPTER 11: CULTIVATE THE EARTH

1. J. Richard Middleton, *The Liberating Image* (Grand Rapids: Brazos, 2005), 26–27, 55, 88–89, 121, 145.
2. Martin Luther, as quoted in Roland Bainton, *Here I Stand* (New York: Abingdon-Cokesbury, 1950), 59.

3. Martin Luther, "Preface to the Complete Edition of Luther's Latin Writings" (Wittenberg, 1545), in *Luther's Works*, ed. Helmut T. Lehman, ed. and trans. John W. Doberstein (Philadelphia: Muhlenberg, 1959), 34:337.
4. Martin Luther, as quoted in Bainton, *Here I Stand*, 65. The source of this quotation is Luther's preface to the 1545 edition of his writings and can be found in *Luther's Works* 34:337.
5. Martin Luther, "The Freedom of a Christian," in *Martin Luther's Basic Theological Writings*, 2nd ed., ed. Timothy F. Lull (Minneapolis: Fortress, 2005), 404–8.

## CHAPTER 12: REST EVERY SEVENTH DAY

1. John Calvin, *The Sermons of M. John Calvin upon the Fifth Booke of Moses Called Deuteronomie*, trans. Arthur Golding (London: 1583; repr., Carlisle, PA: Banner of Truth Trust, 1987), 204. This particular sermon expounds Deuteronomy 5:12–14, the thirty-fourth in Calvin's sermon series on Deuteronomy.
2. William Willimon, *The Pastor: The Theology and Practice of Ordained Ministry* (Nashville: Abingdon, 2000), 329.

## CHAPTER 13: WHAT IS YOUR CALL?

1. David Platt, *Radical* (Colorado Springs: Multnomah, 2010), 78–79.
2. John Piper, *Don't Waste Your Life* (Wheaton: Crossway, 2003), 119–20.
3. Frederick Buechner, *Wishful Thinking: A Theological ABC* (San Francisco: Harper & Row, 1973), 95.
4. I am reluctant to say one calling is higher than another, yet it seems impossible to privilege the pastoral call without implying something like this. What is it that makes the pastoral call special if not the supernatural power required to complete its redemptive task? (Matt. 19:25–26; 2 Tim. 1:6–7; 2:1–10). Elders who pastor well "will receive the crown of glory," a unique reward not promised to any other vocation (1 Peter 5:1–4). There is a reason why ministers of the gospel will "be judged more strictly" (James 3:1; cf. 1 Cor. 3:5–17).

    I attempt to avoid Platonism on one hand and naturalism on the other (the two extremes discussed in chapter 2) by contrasting external activities and internal motivations. Some actions are more important than others, yet all actions that aim at the glory of God are equal before him (Col. 3:23–24).
5. Larry Osborne, *Accidental Pharisees* (Grand Rapids: Zondervan, 2012), 177.
6. Martin Luther, *Sermons of Martin Luther: The Church Postils*, vols. 1 and 2, ed. and trans. John Nicholas Lenker (Grand Rapids: Baker, 1995), 281.

## CHAPTER 14: THE FALL THEN AND NOW

1. Langdon Gilkey, *On Niebuhr* (Chicago: University of Chicago Press, 2001). Gilkey said their rejection of a historical fall arose from their prior commitment to the scientific theory of evolution. He explained, "Every important theologian in the twentieth century accepted this scientific, evolutionary understanding of the past without question, however much most of them studiously avoided refer-

ring to it" (233). Gilkey remembered a telling conversation between Reinhold and Paul Tillich: "Tillich smiled, sighed, and looked at his watch: 'Tell me, Reinnie, when was it, this good creation, and how long did it last? Five minutes, an hour or two, a day? When was it? And if there is no time for your good creation, then can you speak simply of a "story"? Do you not have to speak of a "broken myth" — and are you not then in some mode of ontology, of a discussion of essential nature and its corruption?' Niebuhr knew perfectly well that he had been bested" (94).

2. Ibid., 233–34. See also pp. 134–36.

3. Gilbert K. Chesterton, *Orthodoxy* (New York: John Lane, 1912), 22.

4. For those interested in the debates about original sin, I believe our corruption is passed from parent to child, as Realism teaches, and that our guilt is directly imputed from Adam, according to the Federal Headship view.

5. Gilkey, *On Niebuhr*, 233.

6. The text of Steve Jobs's Stanford commencement speech may be accessed at "'You've Got to Find What You Love,' Jobs Says," *Stanford News* (June 14, 2005), *http://news.stanford.edu/news/2005/june15/jobs-061505.html.*

7. Victor J. Stenger, *The New Atheism* (New York: Prometheus, 2009), 221–22.

8. Theologians who deny a historical fall tend to create a new problem — besides the traditional problems of sin and death — where there isn't one. The Christian gospel is about redemption, which assumes there is something to fix. If there is no fall, then the problem that redemption fixes must lie in creation. If there is no fall, then creation becomes the fall. And our problem, then, is not that we are sinners. It's much worse than that. Our problem is that we exist (cf. Gilkey, *On Niebuhr*, 133: the neoorthodox theologians who denied a historical fall were inclined to see our problem as "an ontological necessity, i.e., that the results of the fall are the consequences of creation").

   We solve the problem of our existence when we overcome our individuality — the part that makes us unique — and lose ourselves in the oneness of God. It is no accident that the same neoorthodox theologians who denied a historical fall also held to a panentheism that ultimately denied the goodness of creation (see John W. Cooper, *Panentheism: The Other God of the Philosophers* [Grand Rapids: Baker Academic, 2006], 206–9). No fall leads to a low view of creation, where rather than restore us as unique image bearers of God, the goal of "redemption" is to return us into the God from which we came.

9. Cited in Gary Strauss, "Ariel Castro Sentenced to Life without Parole," *USA Today* (August 1, 2013), *http://www.usatoday.com/story/news/2013/08/01/castro-sentencing-could-reveal-details-of-kidnap-victims-ordeal/2603725/.*

## CHAPTER 15: THE FALLOUT FROM THE FALL

1. David Platt, *Radical* (Colorado Springs: Multnomah, 2011), 179–81 (emphasis his). Platt confuses things with actions (ontology with ethics) when he writes, "If you and I ever hope to free our lives from worldly desires, worldly thinking, worldly pleasures, worldly dreams, worldly ideals, worldly values, worldly ambitions, and worldly acclaim, then we must focus our lives on another world. Though you and I live in the United States of America now, we must fix our attention on 'a better country — a heavenly one'" (179). We must rid our lives of worldly (read "sin-

ful") pleasures, but not this worldly place. Platt's recommendation seems Platonic, which means he is merely replacing one set of worldly values with another. As I made clear in chapter 2, neither naturalism nor Platonism is Christian.

2. For an honest and hopeful book on death, see Michael Wittmer, *The Last Enemy* (Grand Rapids: Discovery House, 2012).

3. We will learn in the appendix that we must not separate physical and spiritual death, but it does seem necessary to distinguish them.

## CHAPTER 17: GOSPEL

1. David Platt, *Follow Me* (Carol Stream, IL: Tyndale House, 2013), 131 – 32.

2. Bryan Chapell, "What Is the Gospel?" in *The Gospel as Center* (Wheaton: Crossway, 2012), 116.

3. Scot McKnight, *The King Jesus Gospel* (Grand Rapids: Zondervan, 2011), 29 – 32, 37 – 41, 50 – 62, 132 – 34; and N. T. Wright, *What Saint Paul Really Said* (Grand Rapids: Eerdmans, 1997), 40 – 45.

4. "Forgiveness," by TobyMac, featuring Lecrae, © 2012 ForeFront Records.

5. "Fire Fall Down," Hillsong, © 2009.

6. D. Martyn Lloyd-Jones, *Preaching and Preachers* (Grand Rapids: Zondervan, 1972), 68.

7. Michael F. Bird, *Evangelical Theology* (Grand Rapids: Zondervan, 2013), 52.

## CHAPTER 18: KINGDOM

1. Kenneth Bailey, "Through Peasant Eyes," in *Poet & Peasant and Through Peasant Eyes* (Grand Rapids: Eerdmans, 1983), 169.

2. The chorus continues: "And it shows when we stand, hand in hand, make our dreams come true!" (Disney, © 2006). This last, hyperventilating phrase seems to be required in all Disney songs.

3. *Organic* was a popular term in the nineteenth century, much like *paradigm*, *existential*, and well, *organic* are today. We use *organic* to distinguish *natural* food that was grown without chemical fertilizers or pesticides. Kuyper and his era used *organic* to imply the subject was alive (it was a living organism), in contradistinction to the rigid, machinelike notions of the Enlightenment.

4. Kuyper thought that associations of Christian doctors, lawyers, educators, and those of other professions might demonstrate the power of the Christian worldview and attract others to submit to Jesus' universal reign.

5. John Bolt explains: "In Kuyper's view, Christians who go out into their various vocations do so neither as direct emissaries of the institutional church nor as mere individual believers.... Christian social, cultural, and political action does not flow directly from structures and authorities of the church, but comes to expression organically in the various spheres of life as believers live out the faith and spirituality that develops and is nurtured in the church's worship and discipline." See John Bolt, *A Free Church, A Holy Nation: Abraham Kuyper's American Public Theology* (Grand Rapids: Eerdmans, 2000), 428 – 29.

6. Tertullian, "Apology," in *The Ante-Nicene Fathers*, vol. 3, ed. Alexander Roberts and James Donaldson (Edinburgh: T&T Clark; repr., Grand Rapids: Eerdmans, 1973). See chaps. 30, 39, and 44.

7. Rodney Stark, *The Rise of Christianity* (San Francisco: HarperSanFrancisco, 1997), 6–10, 73–94.

8. J. Stevenson, ed., *Creeds, Councils and Controversies*, rev. W. H. C. Frend (London: SPCK, 1989), 57. Julian combatted Christian generosity by instituting a faith-based initiative, giving public assistance to Hellenistic shrines so they could help the needy and win converts to the pagan religion. He wrote to a pagan priest: "I have provided means to meet the necessary expenditure, and have issued directions throughout the whole of Galatia, that you should be furnished annually with thirty thousand bushels of corn and sixty thousand measures of wine, of which the fifth part is to be devoted to the support of the poor who attend upon the priests; and the rest to be distributed among strangers and our own poor. For, while there are no persons in need among the Jews, and while even the impious Galileans [Christians] provide not only for those of their own party who are in want, but also for those who hold with us, it would indeed be disgraceful if we were to allow our own people to suffer from poverty." This letter is recorded by the ancient historian, Sozomen. See "Sozomenus," in *Nicene and Post-Nicene Fathers*, vol. 2, ed. Philip Schaff and Henry Wace (Edinburgh: T&T Clark; repr., Grand Rapids: Eerdmans, 1989): 5:16 (p. 338).

## Chapter 19: Already but Not Yet

1. Albert M. Wolters, *Creation Regained*, 2nd ed. (Grand Rapids: Eerdmans, 1985, 2005), 73 (emphasis his).

2. Cornelius Plantinga Jr., *Engaging God's World* (Grand Rapids: Eerdmans, 2002), 113 (emphasis mine).

3. Ibid., 114 (emphasis mine).

4. Another seminal Dutch Reformed thinker who argues for a single kingdom is Geerhardus Vos. See *The Teaching of Jesus Concerning the Kingdom of God and the Church* (Eugene, OR: Wipf & Stock, 1998), 162–63: "There is a sphere of science, a sphere of art, a sphere of the family and of the state, a sphere of commerce and industry. Whenever one of these spheres comes under the controlling influence of the principle of the divine supremacy and glory, and this outwardly reveals itself, there we can truly say that the kingdom of God has become manifest."

5. Calvin Van Reken, "Christians in This World: Pilgrims or Settlers?" *Calvin Theological Journal* 43 (2008): 234–56, esp. pp. 244–50.

6. For example, see the resolutions for 2013 Synod of the United Church of Christ at "Resolutions and Other Formal Motions from General Synod 29," God's Vision: Love (June 23–July 2, 2013), *http://www.ucc.org/synod/resolutions/*.

7. Michael Horton, "How the Kingdom Comes," *Christianity Today* 50, no. 1 (January 1, 2006): 44–45, *http://www.christianitytoday.com/ct/2006/january/2.43.html*.

8. Michael Horton, "How to Discover Your Calling," *Modern Reformation* (May–June 1999), 9.

9. David Van Drunen, *Living in God's Two Kingdoms* (Wheaton: Crossway, 2010), 26–28.

10. A helpful summary of the two positions and example of mutual critique is Timothy Keller, *Center Church* (Grand Rapids: Zondervan, 2012), 194–245.

## CHAPTER 20: NEW EARTH

1. David Van Drunen, *Living in God's Two Kingdoms* (Wheaton: Crossway, 2010), 62 – 70. He explains, *"This present world was never meant to exist forever ... creation is not seeking an improvement of its present existence but the attainment of its original destiny. It longs to give way before the new heaven and new earth"* (p. 62, emphasis his). Kevin DeYoung and Greg Gilbert caution Kuyperians who wonder whether this or that cultural product will make it from this world into the next. See their *What Is the Mission of the Church?* (Wheaton: Crossway, 2011), 218 – 19.
2. Daniel B. Wallace, "Novum Testamentum Graece," *Journal of the Evangelical Society* (March 2013), 155.
3. For a helpful analysis of this passage, see Al Wolters, "Worldview and Textual Criticism in 2 Peter 3:10," *Westminster Theological Journal* 49 (1987): 405 – 13.
4. The distinction between this age and the next also appears in Matthew 13:39 – 40, 49; Mark 10:30; Luke 18:30; 20:34 – 35; and Ephesians 1:21; 2:7.
5. Irenaeus, *Adversus Haereses*, 5.35 – 36 and 36.1. While Irenaeus rightly noted the distinction between things and actions, he did not fully escape his residual Platonism. He argued that some redeemed humans will be privileged to live in the new heaven while others remain stuck on the new earth.

## CHAPTER 21: CONSUMMATION

1. Kevin DeYoung and Greg Gilbert, *What Is the Mission of the Church?* (Wheaton: Crossway, 2011), 217 – 29; and Owen Strachan, "Is Christic Reconciliation of All Things in Colossians 1 a Mandate for Rehabilitative Creation Care?" *Journal of the Evangelical Theological Society*, November 14, 2012.
2. Gordon D. Fee, *The First Epistle to the Corinthians*, New International Commentary on the New Testament (Grand Rapids: Eerdmans, 1987), 785 – 802. Also see N. T. Wright, *The Resurrection of the Son of God* (Minneapolis: Fortress, 2003), 347 – 56.
3. Thomas Aquinas, *Summa Theologiae*, 1a.97.3 (New York: Blackfriars and McGraw-Hill, 1964), 13:143 – 45.
4. While I appreciate why he would want to believe this, one of the men sent to recover Jim Elliot and his four martyred friends expressed a view of the human body that was too low. He wrote, "I got over my feeling of hating to touch the bodies, because a body is only a house and these fellows had left their house and, after the soul leaves, the body isn't much after all." See Elisabeth Elliot, *Through Gates of Splendor* (1957; rev. 1981, repr., Wheaton: Tyndale House, 1996), 237.
5. Rick Warren, *The Purpose Driven Life* (Grand Rapids: Zondervan, 2002), 49.

## CHAPTER 22: WHAT NOW?

1. James Rowe, "I Would Be Like Jesus," 1912, public domain.
2. John E. Bode, "O Jesus, I Have Promised," 1868, public domain.
3. Johnson Oatman Jr., "Higher Ground," 1898, public domain.

4. Harriet E. Buell, "A Child of the King," 1877, public domain.
5. James M. Black, "When the Roll Is Called Up Yonder," 1893, public domain.
6. Eliza E. Hewitt, "When We All Get to Heaven," 1898, public domain.
7. Luther B. Bridgers, "He Keeps Me Singing," 1910, public domain.
8. Isaac Watts and Robert Lowry (refrain), "We're Marching to Zion," 1707 (refrain, 1867), public domain.
9. Albert E. Brumley, "I'll Fly Away" (Hartford Music Co, 1932; Albert E. Brumley and Sons, 1960).
10. Richard Blanchard, "Fill My Cup, Lord" (1959; Sacred Songs, 1964, 1975).

## Appendix: Partial Fall?

1. N. T. Wright, "The Letter to the Romans," in *The New Interpreter's Bible* (Nashville: Abingdon, 2002), 10:526.
2. Thomas Long, *Accompany Them with Singing: The Christian Funeral* (Louisville: Westminster John Knox, 2009), 38 – 41.
3. Even some conservative theologians suggest that physical death is natural to humans because we are inherently mortal. Our "physical death is a part of the natural life cycle" and not a consequence of sin. See Gerald Bray, *God Is Love* (Wheaton: Crossway, 2012), 376 – 77, 234 – 35.
4. Abraham Kuyper, *Lectures on Calvinism* (1931; repr., Grand Rapids: Eerdmans, 1999), 131 – 36.